The Building and Saving of a Railway
By Martin Pearson

An account of the national and local decisions that led to the building of the Settle-Carlisle Railway, a story about the twists and turns in its fortunes, including the successful attempt to resist almost certain closure in the 1980s with official documents explaining why the line was saved.

Preface

This book is a case study of decision making from 1850-1990 as it affected the Settle-Carlisle Railway. There are many twists and turns in that saga.

Against expectations the Government on 11th April 1989 decided to refuse British Rail's request to close the line. Since then it has stayed open and thrived. The key Ministers were Paul Channon, Secretary of State and Michael Portillo, Minister of State.

Using the Freedom of Information Act I have been able to unearth a number of original documents which shed light on the actual decision by Government, including the crucial letter written by Paul Channon to Mrs Thatcher on 6th April 1989. He told her of his recommendation to reprieve the line. We also have the formal Civil Service Assessment that was sent to Mr Portillo on 24th February 1989. On balance it recommended closure but accepted that the facts of the case could be used to justify either closure or retention.

This means this is as near the official record as one can get of what really happened. I hope it trumps the speculation of the intervening years. In addition there are two letters, one from Edward Album on behalf of the Friends of the Settle-Carlisle Line to Lord Whitelaw, and the other from Ruth Annison, on behalf of the Business Liaison Group to Mrs Thatcher presenting her petition. Both letters illustrate the quality of arguments used by protesters and their contribution to a successful result. This book includes these papers as appendices.

In terms of understanding decision making I used a model developed by Graham Allison who had explored the Cuban Missile crisis in some depth. I have tried to focus on an understanding of decision making, rather than the individuals concerned.

The case study also provides a short 100 year national railway history perspective which helps to understand the circumstances which led up to the appointment of Dr Beeching.

Where there are inconsistencies in the published record I have provided an analysis of some of the issues, for instance the possible role of Heritage in the final decision making as no reference at all is made to this in the Paul Channon letter.

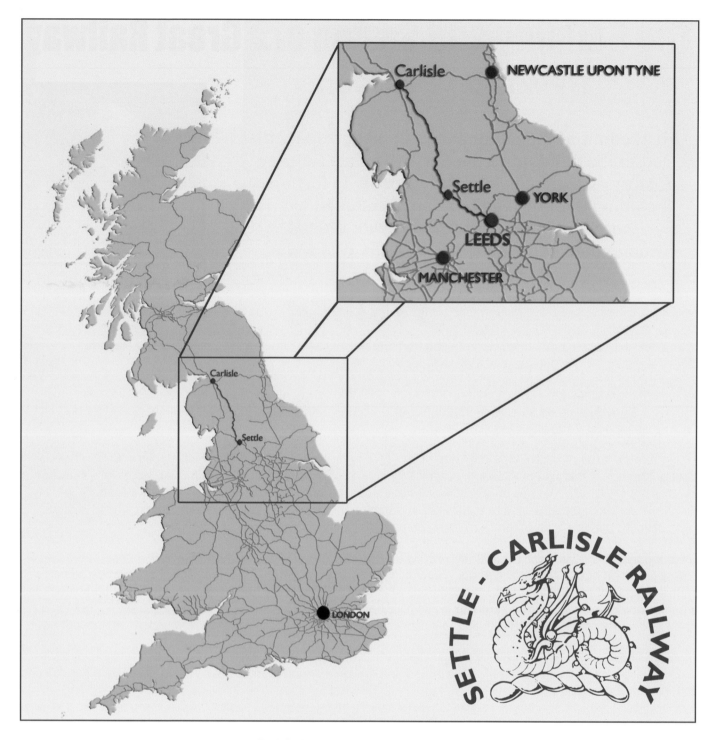

Published by Martin Pearson
23 Town Head, Settle, North Yorkshire, BD24 9JB
(Please make cheques payable to J. M. Pearson)

© **Martin Pearson 2016**

All rights reserved
No part of this publication may be reproduced or transmitted in
any form or by any means without the prior written permission of the publisher

ISBN   978 0 9955652 0 3

British Library Cataloguing in Publication Data
A catalogue record for this book is available from the British Library

Design and Layout: Castle Communications of Solihull, West Midlands
With further work by ImageRail

Printed by PDS Print, Plympton, Plymouth, PL7 4LU

Contents

Introduction

The background to this case study of decision making

This work started out as a case study into decision making as it affected the Settle-Carlisle Railway over a 130 year period. The trigger for this was an MP in the news for receiving payments for asking questions on behalf of the government of Fiji. This is an example of bad lobbying.

A thought arose. **The line would not be open if other railway companies and landowners had not lobbied Parliament in 1869 when the Midland Railway Company tried to get out of its obligations? What if the 1980s campaign had failed? There could be good lobbying as well as bad.**

Later the focus moved away from lobbying to decision making. Decision making in government or in any organisation is not necessarily a straightforward rational process as some would have us believe. Politics with a small *p* or large *P* can be involved but so too are factors which just go with the systems and routines of decision makers.

When doing an Open University degree with a module on Decision Making, I came across a book by Graham T Allison who looked at the Cuban Missile Crisis through three prisms:
- The Rational Actor - The classical way in which decisions are made
- Government or Bureaucracy Political Model
- Organisational Process Model

Some illustrations of the models are set out in Appendix 1, where examples such as the Jupiter Missiles in Turkey, the Naval Blockade, the identification of the missiles in Cuba and plans by the USSR to construct the missile sites are examined.

Throwing light on the Settle-Carlisle Line decisions

In applying these principles to the Settle-Carlisle Line it may be possible to rescue some reputations and to throw light on to the decision by the government to reprieve the line in 1989.

A national perspective

I have included an analysis of key national railway decisions over the period. This enables the reader to have a grasp of why the country found itself in the late 1950s with a railway service that was running with losses of £300,000 per day.

Freedom of Information Act

Extensive enquiries have been made using the Freedom of Information Act. A brief summary of my experience is set out on page 34. I have been dealt with politely but the decision making within different agencies or departments varies a lot. However in December 2015 and subsequently the Department of Transport did release some key documents, including the letter written by Paul Channon, the Secretary of State, to Mrs Thatcher on 6th April 1989 telling her of his decision to reprieve the line and some internal legal arguments.

The Department of Transport has been rather like a curate's egg. It was positive (with the help of The National Archives at Kew), when they agreed that 18 closed files should be re-opened with some redactions. It is also good that they have released the Paul Channon letter and some legal advice around the issue of bus substitution given in late March 1989. An extra document contains legal arguments on a draft letter approving the closure of the line, which shows how close we came to a contrary decision.

In the last few weeks the DfT have released further information including the final submission made by the Civil Service to Michael Portillo and Paul Channon on 24th February 1989. This has been very helpful but further information has yet to be released.

Paul Channon letter

The Paul Channon letter which is reproduced here means that there are a number of primary source documents in this book. Access to other primary documents has been obtained, which need to be properly followed up.

Who made the final decision?

It is not yet possible to ascertain from official records if the decision was made within the Department of Transport or came after outside intervention. **Michael Portillo, Minister of State, at the time is very clear that the matter had been settled in government before Paul Channon wrote to the Prime Minister. It is clear that crucial decisions came from the Department for Transport, but they were expecting a favourable response from No. 10.**

Other documents show serious attempts to sell the line to a private bidder or a consortium. Deep criticism of this process from campaigners was necessary up to the final days in order to secure a successful result.

Martin Pearson

Foreword by Michael Portillo

Long after my political career had come to a spectacular end - I lost my seat in what Guardian readers and Channel 4 viewers voted their third favourite moment of the 20th century - I was asked what had been my greatest achievement. I knew that the interviewer was expecting some macro policy in the realm of national finance or defence. "Saving the Settle to Carlisle line" took him by surprise, which was what I had intended.

I hasten to add that I was not claiming sole ownership of the act. Many others were involved in the happy outcome. But as I looked back, I reflected that it was one of those decisions that could have gone either way, and the result bore my fingerprints.

I became Minister of State for Transport in summer 1988. I succeeded David Mitchell, a man of old fashioned good manners who, having been "let go" in the reshuffle, lingered in the department in order to brief me on the portfolio. "You have to save the Settle Carlisle", he said.

That may seem surprising since the government had recently announced, in response to British Rail's application to close the line, that it was "minded" to accede. That was because the administration was tiptoeing through a minefield of legal booby-traps. Loss-making lines could be supported with a subsidy - public service obligation grants - but only for defined purposes. British Rail, under pressure from the government to reduce its losses, had offered a gloomy scenario of a route that made severe losses because passengers scarcely used it; and the problem would get worse because the infrastructure - particularly the celebrated Ribblehead viaduct - was in need of heavy investment. The government's announcement had invited representations and focused minds.

I was quite unnerved by the issue. The politics of northern England were pretty clear even to a southerner like me. In any case, the line was a thing of beauty, a part of the national heritage and a monument to those many who had died building it in the 1870s. Surreptitiously, I ventured forth to see it for myself, alighting incognito from the sleeper at Carlisle so as to ride the route south, in the cab of the diesel. The presence of a television camera at 6am shook me. As the sun rose on the train moving south, the stations and bridges were crowded with demonstrators with banners that welcomed me by name. Clearly the Friends of the Settle to Carlisle had friends in the department, and had received a leak!

The Friends were evidently effective and serious. That made it a pleasure to engage with them. But it also meant that we had to be wary of a real prospect of legal challenge by them or by local authorities if we put a foot wrong. I had to maintain a poker face, even as I sought to find a solution that would keep the trains running.

I had high hopes of a privatisation. After all, at least some in British Rail wanted to be rid of the services. They ran few trains and some intermediate stations had closed. An operator with enthusiasm and imagination might structure and market the services properly. At times we seemed to be near to such a solution, but legal problems and a lack of investor confidence frustrated the efforts of both British Rail and the government.

Two developments turned the tide. First, Tony Freschini, the line engineer, proposed a different method for tackling the Ribblehead viaduct repairs, and his cost estimate was dramatically lower than the figure in British Rail's case for closure. Second, thanks to the Friends and other campaign groups, the numbers using the line rose steeply. The financial case for closure now looked weaker.

Martin Pearson has in this book unearthed key documents from the period. On 6th April 1989 the Secretary of State for Transport, Paul Channon, wrote to the Prime Minister, Margaret Thatcher, proposing that the closure application be refused. The letter is interesting because it reflects all the legal hazards to which the government felt exposed. Our wish to save the line had to be rational, reasonable, and judge-proof.

Of course, the whole thing had been settled within government before the letter was sent. I have to rely on my memory for what had happened. My recollection is that Mrs Thatcher was not anti railway as people supposed, but she was a conservative, that is to say one who valued our heritage very much. She had no particular wish to antagonise Cumbria and Yorkshire, and she was fond of Willie Whitelaw, who had been MP for Penrith and the Border until June 1983 and was deputy prime minister (in the Lords) until early 1988. We needed thoroughly to make the case to save the line, but we were pushing an open door to Number 10.

This book will be of interest to those who were involved in the campaign, and to those who enjoy the line today. More widely, it provides an insight into how government works. People may be surprised by how constrained is an administration's freedom of manoeuvre, and how many legal niceties must be observed.

About twenty years after the reprieve I travelled on a steam train along the line in new circumstances, making the first series of "Great British Railway Journeys" for BBC2. The valleys and bridges were crowded with people watching, filming and photographing the train. It was indeed a superb sight. I felt deep emotion as I considered that the line might have closed. What a terrible loss that would have been.

In my letter to the Friends announcing the reprieve back in 1989 I asked them to live up to the promises that they had made. They have. The community is strongly invested in the line, and the intermediate stations are superbly maintained, decked out in nostalgia and flowers.

I believe that the Settle to Carlisle journey could be better marketed still. My own hobbyhorse is that the trains should be glass roofed. That's how Swiss railways announce to passengers that they are in for a visual treat. But that is a battle for the future. I fought mine more than a quarter of a century ago.

Michael Portillo
October 2016

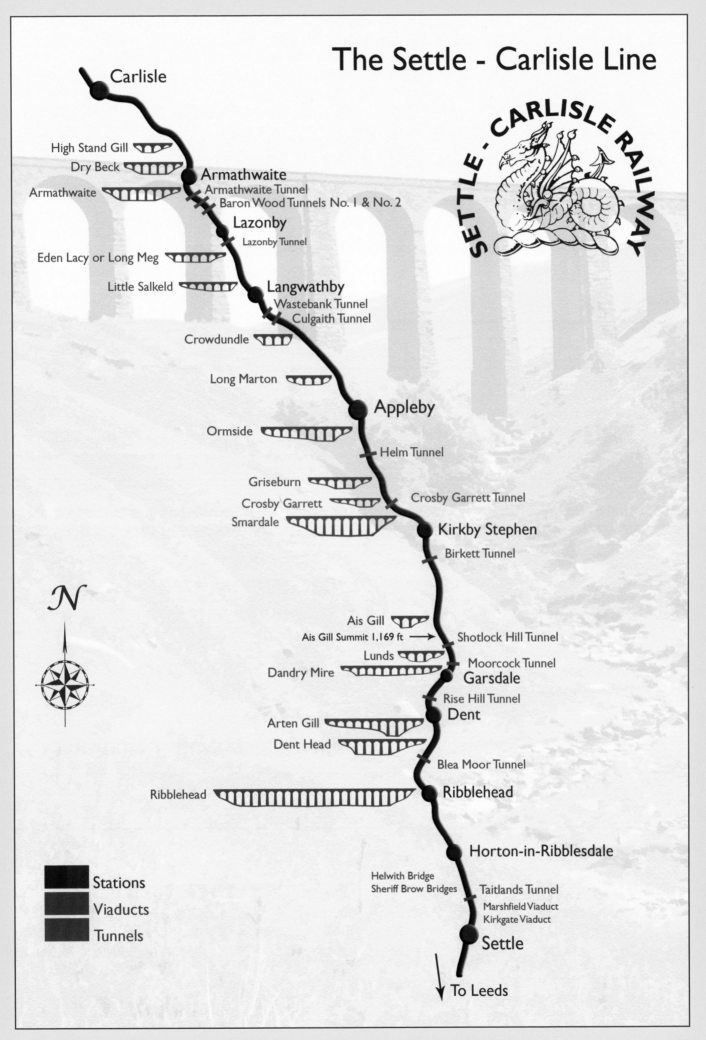

The Settle - Carlisle Line

SETTLE - CARLISLE RAILWAY

Carlisle

High Stand Gill
Dry Beck
Armathwaite
Armathwaite
Armathwaite Tunnel
Baron Wood Tunnels No. 1 & No. 2
Lazonby
Lazonby Tunnel
Eden Lacy or Long Meg
Little Salkeld
Langwathby
Wastebank Tunnel
Culgaith Tunnel
Crowdundle
Long Marton
Appleby
Ormside
Helm Tunnel
Griseburn
Crosby Garrett
Crosby Garrett Tunnel
Smardale
Kirkby Stephen
Birkett Tunnel

N

Ais Gill
Ais Gill Summit 1,169 ft → Shotlock Hill Tunnel
Lunds
Moorcock Tunnel
Dandry Mire
Garsdale
Rise Hill Tunnel
Dent
Arten Gill
Dent Head
Blea Moor Tunnel
Ribblehead
Ribblehead

Horton-in-Ribblesdale

Helwith Bridge
Sheriff Brow Bridges
Taitlands Tunnel
Marshfield Viaduct
Kirkgate Viaduct

Stations
Viaducts
Tunnels

Settle

To Leeds

CHAPTER 1

Why Settle-Carlisle Railway as a Case Study?

Introducing the Decision Making Model

Case study

To help achieve a true understanding of an event, a case study is a helpful tool in two ways. The first relates to the event itself. A really good example of this is **David Jenkinson** in *Rails in the Fells - A Railway Case Study*, which uses his background as a geographer to illustrate facets of the Settle-Carlisle Line that others do not touch.

The second reason for undertaking a case study is to illustrate how the issues arising and methods used may apply in completely different scenarios. In the case of the Decision Making Model, it means recognising that issues are complex. The old journalistic cliché that everything should be presented as either black or white generally gets in the way of a true story. ***Real experiences are more like 50 shades of grey.***

Settle-Carlisle railway

The story of the Settle-Carlisle Line has its early roots in the 1850s. Before the line was built, Parliament was involved twice. The line opened in 1875. One hundred years later, starting with a Ramblers Special, there was a heroic campaignto save a major railway line from closure - something that no other community or preservation group had done.

There are so many twists and turns of the *Will It? Won't It?* variety *and Yes it Will, No it Won't* that it provides ideal material for a case study. It would be wrong to call it a pantomime but it could make a brilliant soap opera. Those involved in the saga came from so many different backgrounds that the story has significant relevance for today's decision makers.

Decision making model

Graham Allison in his *Essence of Decision - Explaining the Cuban Missile Crisis* argues that a typically curious person - even an analyst - puts himself or herself in place of a nation or national government, or indeed any type of organisation, and asks "Why did so-and so happen?" They then try to figure out why a cause of action was chosen. This assumes that (in the case of governments, for example) the decisions came about as a result of purposive actions. The predominant model thus becomes the Rational Actor. Allison suggests that this takes one only so far but is insufficient and suggests three prisms:

- The Rational Actor - the classical model by which decisions are analysed
- Organisational Process Model
- Government or Bureaucracy Political Model.

These are explained more fully in Appendix 1.

Narrative approach

The case study starts with a narrative approach. Firstly, to understand anything about a local situation it is crucial to set the scene in a national context. By exploring railway history (albeit it with a management perspective) it is possible to understand some of the issues that the UK has in respect of rail transport.

Not a planned railway network

Hopefully, the case study helps debunk some of the simplistic road-v-rail arguments. We can see more clearly why, unlike other countries, we never had a planned national railway network, and we realise that constructing railways in the UK in the 19th century was an expensive business.

Beeching, Marples and so on

For many the debate will start with Dr Beeching, Ernest Marples MP and the quite brilliant campaign against closure in the 1980s. However, if we focus only on that we miss out on:

- The 1866 Financial crisis, which is very like more recent experience in the UK

- Attempts in the 1930s to relieve railway companies from the Common Carrier responsibility
- Attempts to get road users to contribute to highway costs
- Wartime experiences of railways starved of money

In the same way, by putting the 1950s Plan for Modernisation under the microscope we come across Treasury Civil Service mistrust of railway management.

Closure campaign of the 1980s

The campaign against closure is examined at some length. In particular, there were three sets of tactical decisions made by BR which rebounded on them spectacularly. Twenty five years after the event I examine the different perspectives - in particular, the reasons for the apparent change of Government thought between May 1988 when the Secretary of State was "minded to close" and the reprieve 11 months later.

Three possible explanations for the reprieve are explored:

- One is the argument that the Government had to admit defeat as no other options existed

- The other two examine "raw politics" and the transport of imported coal as significant factors, if not in the decision making itself, but to account for the later alacrity with which action was taken

Finally, one could well ask why the railway industry has been poor at lobbying **(FoSCL and Joint Action Committee excepted!).** However, that interesting question falls outside the remit of this case study.

CHAPTER 2 PART 1
National and Local Narrative 1850-1880
Birth of a Railway

Setting the scene - National

Rapid railway expansion in middle of the 19th century

The great era of railway expansion was 1830-1850. By 1838, 5.5 million passengers were being carried. By 1845 it was 30 million and by 1855 111 million. By 1875 this had exploded to 490 million. The miles of track rose from 500 in 1838 to 5,000 ten years later and by 1860 there were 10,000 miles of railway.

Parliamentary reform: a growing electorate

Parliament consists of two Houses. The House of Commons (referred to as Parliament) and the House of Lords. The first reform of the Commons had taken place in 1832. Not only did this remove "rotten boroughs" but it led to the end of the over-representation of the countryside and small market towns.

An old electorate of 435,000 had risen to 650,000. By 1866 it had risen to just over a million and the following year, after more reforms, it was nearly 2 million. One in three men could vote. There were still about 650 MPs, with over 100 from Ireland. England had 456, Scotland 60 and Wales 33.

The background of MPs changed only slowly. In 1833, 217 MPs were sons of peers or were baronets. By 1860, this was 180 and by 1889 down to 170.

Parliament and the railways: regulation

Between 1849 and 1893 Parliament passed eight railway regulation acts. In 1840 the Board of Trade was given responsibility for some oversight. A Railways Board, the equivalent of Her Majesty's Railway Inspectors, was also created.

Probably the most significant Act was the 1844 Railway Act promoted by Gladstone when President of the Board of Trade. It was the first time Parliament had put an overarching roof over rail companies. It contained an option for nationalisation 21 years later of any company formed after 1844.

Crucially, it created "Parliamentary Trains". One train a day - each way - had to stop at every station and it had to have a third class carriage for which the rate charged was 1 penny (d) per mile.

Not allowing for all line discounts, the trip from Settle to Carlisle would have been six shillings. However, Jenkinson points out that the average all-line local fare was probably about 1s 4d. From **Peter Baughan** in Midland Railway North of Leeds - The Leeds-Settle-Carlisle Line and its branches we learn that in 1870 the day rate for a carpenter was 6s and that of a labourer just 4s 6d.

If a company wished to promote a railway, a Private Act of Parliament was needed. By 1860 the requirements of the Acts were contained in about 48 sections. **Stan Abbott and Alan Whitehouse** - The Line that Refused to Die - make clear that although Parliament sanctioned the acquisition of land, railway development was never done in a co-ordinated way. Parliament's fear of monopoly led to much unnecessary duplication.

Parliament and the railways: individual companies

In the period 1825-35, Parliament approved 54 Railway Acts. From 1836-37 there were 39 more. In 1846 The Midland Railway itself gave sanction to 26 more Bills. The number of companies at any one time was affected by mergers but by 1922 there were still 120 railway companies.

Each Act was scrutinised by a Committee of MPs who would then make a recommendation to Parliament. Whilst individuals could give evidence in their own right, it was the practice for the principal parties to employ counsel who could cross-examine witnesses.

Allegedly, this meant that the process was open to bribery - either from the sponsors or the opponents - who in the early days were the canal and turnpike companies and coach operators.

Up to 150 MPs seem to have been on railway company payrolls. Other lobbyists for the railways were coal owners keen to get better access to the country and, of course, some landowners.

Cost of railways

Landowners had realised that they could make money from the railways and it was not long before they were charging up to £40,000 per mile. Bear in mind that the rental the Midland Railway paid to use King's Cross was £20,000 per annum or £1,615,476 at 2013 levels.

This meant that building railways in the UK was more expensive than elsewhere. The 1860 costs per mile were:

- UK   £54,142
- England and Wales   £64,453
- Prussia   £21,000
- United States   £13,000

On this basis the Midland Railway company planned to build the Settle-Carlisle at £30,565 per mile. It came in at £48,611 per mile. The total cost was £290 million at 2013 prices.

Locomotive Acts

Attempts to develop self-propelled motor vehicles began in the 18th century. Initially, it related to steam traction and quite large vehicles dominated the highways.

It was inevitable that Parliament would legislate. And it did in 1861, 1865 and 1878. The most draconian Act was that of 1865. The law required every power-driven vehicle on the roads to have a man in front 60 yards ahead. During daylight hours he had to carry a red flag and a lantern at night.

The motor car itself did not emerge until 1886 and there is a dispute as to whether or not railway companies had undue influence. This law was not abolished until 1895, when restrictions were lifted and an upper speed of 14 mph introduced.

Setting the scene – Northern England into Scotland

A number of railway companies are relevant to the story about ways in which to get through traffic from England to Scotland and, of course, vice versa.

Midland Railway, London and North Western Railway and the Euston Square Confederacy

The Midland Railway, which was Derby-based, found that it was sandwiched between two rival routes north from London. What later became known as the West Coast Main Line was under the control of London and North Western Railway (LNWR) and Caledonian, whilst the putative East Coast Line was run by Great Northern Railway, North Eastern Railway, and North British.

The Midland was keen to secure access to Scotland. Its own access was via the "Little North Western", which it controlled to Ingleton. The Ingleton Branch Line to Low Gill was controlled by LNWR. At Low Gill it joined the Lancaster and Carlisle Railway, also under LNWR control.

The two companies had not always been at loggerheads. Around 1850 they had combined with the Manchester, Sheffield and Lincolnshire Railway against the Great Northern in what became known as the Euston Square Confederacy. It was in effect a cartel.

William Gladstone restores order

Great Northern retaliated at the time of the Great Exhibition. The Midland responded with virtually free travel via their route. It took William Gladstone MP, who knew people from his time at the Board of Trade, to restore order.

Earlier, Captain Mark Huish (LNWR) had proposed a merger which John Ellis, Midland Railway pioneer, had declined. In 1852 a three-way scheme for union with the Great Northern was put to Parliament but rejected quickly on monopoly grounds. However, over the years relationships declined, primarily over disputes about London stations, and their rivalry intensified.

The key decision-making Midland Railway individuals were William Evans Hutchinson, Chairman 1864-70; William Price, Chairman 1870-73; and James Allport, General Manager. LNWR were represented by Richard Moon, who was Chairman from 1861-1891 and knighted in 1887; and William Cawkwell, General Manager from 1858-75.

Hutchinson, like many others in railway management or ownership, was a Quaker. He played a significant role in the Abandonment Bill. William Philip Price, 1817-91, was Liberal MP for Gloucester. He was Deputy Chairman from 1864-70 and Chairman from 1870-73. He came from Tibberton Court and was a nonconformist heir to a timber importing business.

Later during the construction of the Settle-Carlisle Line shareholders were quite vocal. William Price stood down and the post of Chairman was taken over by Edward Shipley Ellis (son of the railway pioneer John Ellis), who himself was a Leicester City Councillor, Alderman and JP.

Having stood down, Price became a railway commissioner in 1873, overseeing the Railway Act of 1854. James Allport (1811-1892) had worked at Birmingham and Derby Junction, leaving in 1839 when the Midland Railway Company took over. He came back to the Midland Railway in October 1853 as General Manager. He joined the Board for three years before returning to his job as General Manager. Later he re-joined the Board and became Chairman.

Caledonian: keen to retain the only rail route to Scotland

The Caledonian Railway company in Scotland, with its partner LNWR, had a virtual monopoly of west coast traffic to Glasgow and Edinburgh. If the Midland Railway obtained an independent route to Carlisle, the LNWR/Caledonian monopoly would be broken.

North British: constructors of the Tay and Forth Bridges

North British was an Edinburgh-based company keen to link their city with the south. They were an ally of the Midland Railway Company. It was they who built the Tay Bridge in 1878, which collapsed a year later. It was rebuilt within 10 years. In addition, they and other railway companies - including the Midland - built the Forth Bridge and other important viaducts. The key individual here is Lord William Hay, who took over as Chairman in 1866. He was a Liberal MP for Taunton, later becoming Marquis of Tweeddale.

Glasgow and South Western

A Glasgow-based company, it eventually became an ally of the Midland. Glasgow St Enoch's station was closely modelled on St Pancras. One key individual is Sir James Lumsden. A director from 1849, he was Chairman from 1870-1879 and Lord Provost of Glasgow in 1866.

Lancashire and Yorkshire

Lancashire and Yorkshire Railway also supported the line. They wanted traffic from Liverpool and Manchester to feed into the Midland Line at Hellifield for better access to Scotland. We shall see later how significant their involvement was.

Ingleton and Scotland: an episode of brinksmanship and passengers walking between two stations

The brinkmanship over transfer of passengers at Ingleton is well described by **Michael Pearson** in *Pearson's Railway Guides - Leeds-Settle-Carlisle* and **Martin Bairstow** in *The "Little" North Western Railway*, and by many others. Back in 1855 Parliament had accepted an argument that building a railway between Ingleton and Low Gill was in the public interest. Built by the Lancaster and Carlisle railway and financed by LNWR, it cost the Midland Railway Company nothing.

In 1861 The Midland reopened the Clapham - Ingleton Line as double track and shortly afterwards replaced their temporary station at Ingleton with a permanent one. LNWR continued to terminate the other side of the viaduct.

Suffice it to say that passengers were made to walk between two stations, often involving a descent of 80 feet to the River Greta and a climb to the top. Even when some agreements were made to stop this, the resulting connecting trains could only be described as laughable. Midland passengers also had problems at Tebay.

A worthless deal

LNWR and Midland continued to talk. LNWR proposed a joint line between Ingleton and Carlisle. The Midland wanted freedom to set its own fares and this was agreed except for traffic stopping intermediately on the line. However, LNWR excluded Carlisle Citadel from the equation and, since all the Midland traffic would stop at Carlisle, the deal was worthless.

Settle and Carlisle 1865-1866: Parliament says YES

In the end, the Midland Railway came up with a plan. It was to build a route directly to Carlisle. Here, its positive relationship with North British would give it access to Edinburgh. A route to Glasgow could come about because of links to the Glasgow and South Western Railway.

The route was to start at Settle Junction on the "Little" North Western Line and end at Petteril Bridge Junction outside Carlisle on the Newcastle-Carlisle Line of the North Eastern Railway, which later became a Midland ally. This had opened in 1839. So the final mile was to be over North Eastern metals.

However, even before it got this far the Midland Railway had to subvert a proposal from the North of England Union Railway for an 88-mile route between two industrial areas. Although primarily for freight, it could have been a significant rival. Several Midland Board Directors were behind it. Suffice it to say that as early as 31st March 1865 the Midland Railway had taken over the Bill and by 29th June the Bill was formally suspended.

Feasibility study from Carlisle to Settle: walking most of the route and meeting the 'Man from Tasmania'

James Allport (54) and John Crossley (52), Chief Engineer, undertook a feasibility study. They had probably assessed that they would need to use the Eden and Ribble valleys. Some information for part of the route came from Ordnance Survey sheets. They had done similar work before in the Peak District.

They walked most of the route from Carlisle to Settle, possibly staying at Appleby, the Moorcock Inn and Gearstones. Quite when they came across Charles Stanley Sharland is unclear. Sharland was the 20-year old "Man from Tasmania" who led the preliminary survey of the line. They may have met him in July just as he was leaving the Maryport and Carlisle Railway Company.

On 2nd August the Midland Board gave the go ahead to Crossley to proceed with surveys. The timetable that Allport was working against was to get all papers and documentation to Parliament by 30th November 1865 if the Bill was to be considered in the next Parliamentary year. This was very challenging.

Kenneth Duffin - *The Man from Tasmania* - describes in detail how Charles Stanley Sharland was to walk the 72 miles from Carlisle to Settle taking flying surveys and levels to get a broad idea of what engineering was involved. He did this in 10 days with a small team with him.

Instructions from Allport to Sharland

The instructions that Sharland received from Allport would have related to straight lines and a gradient not in excess of 1:100. Allport would have been most interested in the relationship to the valley floor. His biggest problem was to find a way into and then out of Dentdale.

We do not know whether or not Allport and Crossley were waiting for Sharland at the end of the survey, but the idea of them meeting up at The Golden Lion in Settle before rushing off to Derby is intriguing.

The project that was finally presented was one with four railways. The first started south of Settle terminating at Hawes - 28 miles. The second railway - implied as a branch line - was across Garsdale Common to Appleby and was for 20 miles. The third line was from Appleby to Petteril Bridge Junction. The final link to Carlisle was never built as MR and North Eastern Railway reached agreement over use of NER track.

Parliamentary opposition to the Bill, plus supporters and opponents outside

Within Parliament the Bill was vigorously opposed by the London and North Western Railway, who argued that the public interest was already adequately served by the Ingleton route. The Caledonian Railway also opposed the Bill. The route was supported by Glasgow and South Western, North British and Lancashire and Yorkshire.

The Bill also had its supporters, notably villages and towns in the Eden Valley. Indeed, Appleby went wild with excitement as soon as the Bill had passed the House of Commons.

Parliament was not persuaded to protect the LNWR monopoly and on July 16th 1866 the Midland Railway (Settle and Carlisle) Bill became an Act.

1866-1869 - The Missing Years – or Ducks on Water

Royal Assent to the Bill but nothing much happening on the ground

Within three months of Royal Assent having been given to the Bill, John Crossley, Chief Engineer, was instructed to stake out the line. However, not a lot appeared be happening. A year after instructions had been given to Crossley, staking out was still incomplete, although some tenders were received by October 1868. This was because of two financial crises which created shareholder concern.

Overend, Gurney and Company - the banker's bank

A highly significant bank was Overend, Gurney and Company. Built on extremely sound financial principles, it had been led by Samuel Gurney, a Quaker banker from Norfolk.

The bank had become very important - banks who normally dealt with The Bank of England tended to deal with Overend and Gurney and it was regarded as the "banker's bank". Samuel Gurney retired in 1855 after his wife's death and died in1856. His sister was Elizabeth Fry.

Modern parallels

Immediately after Gurney retired, the Board altered its investment portfolio into what turned out to be more risky areas. In terms of change of policy, there is a parallel with what happened to GEC/Marconi once Lord Weinstock retired after his son's early death. George Simpson ruined the company in five years, losing a cash reserve of £3 billion very quickly.

In terms of wider impact, the Royal Bank of Scotland saga under the leadership of Sir Fred Goodwin is the obvious parallel.

Financial problems - and three men from the Bank of England

Problems came to light in May 1866 when the Midland Railway Bill was nearing its Parliamentary conclusion. On 10th May, Overend & Gurney suspended payments. Three men from the Bank of England in Threadneedle Street went to inspect their books. Overend & Gurney had assumed that the Bank would bail them out. In the end they didn't, preferring short term problems to a full rescue with precedents set for others.

Interest rates up, a bank collapse and railway companies going bust

Gladstone, who was Chancellor of the Exchequer and in on the discussions, raised interest rates to 10%. The Bank collapsed on 11th May and went into liquidation in June 1866, followed by over 200 companies, including railway companies going the same way.

North British: poor track maintenance and a crisis at board level

A second problem emerged in September 1866 when a new Company Secretary revealed that North British - the potential line to Edinburgh - had not been maintaining track, and moreover had paid dividends out of capital. The Chairman and the whole Board of the company resigned and it was then that Lord William Hay took over as Chairman.

Rapprochement and an approach to Parliament

Shareholder unease, more capital needed and land purchases halted

In addition to the two external crises, the Midland Board had to deal with shareholders who were extremely unhappy at the turn of events. There were shareholder meetings every six months. Peter Baughan describes at some length the difficulties that the Board had with shareholders. By December 1867, the Midland Directors needed to raise £5 million capital and on 31st December 1867 decided to defer operations and halt land purchases on the line.

Seeking an agreement over Ingleton

It was against this background that the Midland Railway Company and LNWR sought to reach agreement over Ingleton. Indeed, an approach was made to LNWR by a Shareholder Association without the knowledge of the Midland Board.

The situation in Scotland became complicated as Caledonian and Glasgow and South West sought merger talks. Much energy and expense was involved in seeing these off. LNWR then offered talks on co-operation if the Settle line was abandoned.

At first the Midland declined - but bearing in mind the huge cost of building St Pancras (opened on October 1st 1868) in London and of the difficult Peak Forest Line to Manchester, and recognising its own financial problems, it decided to approach Parliament to abandon the Act. An Abandonment Bill was laid before Parliament in November 1868 for consideration in the 1869 Parliamentary session.

Midland on the horns of a dilemma

However, as Duffin says, the Midland was on the horns of a dilemma. If Parliament accepted the Abandonment Bill, then well and good. If they did not, the authority for compulsory purchase would fall on 16th July 1869 - three years after Royal Assent.

Abandonment Bill reaches the Commons

So, in August 1868, on the advice of solicitors, Midland decided to serve notice of compulsory purchase on landowners. The Abandonment Bill sponsored by Midland Railway and LNWR started its journey through the House of Commons Committee on Thursday, 8th April 1869. The Committee was chaired by Myles William O'Reilly MP. All major parties were represented by legal counsel.

Arguments back and forth, accusations of broken promises, and 40-foot long petition

Peter Baughan describes the ebb and flow of the arguments. Some strong arguments were put forward by Lancashire and Yorkshire, who felt that the abandonment would mean that the Midland had no need to have friendly relations with the company elsewhere.

Lord Wharncliffe came before the Committee to remind them that the Midland would be breaking their promise to build the line, as a result of which the NEU group had agreed to quit the field. North British recited many examples of difficulties for passengers and livestock because of poor relations with LNWR.

Counsel appeared for the landowners, 1,600 of whom had signed a petition wanting the line. The petition (never formerly presented) was on 40 feet of linen in a double column.

The Committee met quite briefly and found that the preamble to the Act had not been proved. Hutchinson, Chairman of the Midland, had argued strongly for the Bill. Shareholders who wanted the abandonment applauded him for his efforts, as did the LNWR Directors.

Members of Parliament, almost pathologically cautious of railway monopoly, had for the second time in 16 years rebuffed the Midland Railway Company.

Building the Railway

Accepting the inevitable and raising money for a start on the line

The Midland Railway Company moved quickly. On 18th May 1869 the Midland Shareholders meeting in Derby accepted the inevitable and did not quibble with the Board. They gave the go-ahead for the company to raise £550,000 towards making a start on the line.

First stone laid at Ribblehead

In the meantime, the Notices to Treat had been issued and were being co-ordinated by Henry Craske Roper. These had to be completed by 16th July 1869. By 14th September 1869 the Midland had let the first contracts for the work, which commenced in November. On 12th October 1870 the first stone was laid at Ribblehead.

Steep climbs out and sharp bends avoided

Abbott and Whitehouse describe in some detail how the Midland Railway Company wanted to get their trains to Scotland by the shortest and quickest route.

Steep climbs were out. Not for them the 1 in 75 LNWR route at Shap Fell, or the 1.37.7 rise on the Lickey incline (Bromsgrove and Blackwell) for 2 miles 4 chains. In the same way, sharp bends needed to be avoided. The ruling gradient was to be 1:100.

Jenkinson explains how curvature can indicate a function of a line. Unless a curve is very gentle, it will impose unacceptable speed limits for main line work. So sharp curves were out.

A masterpiece of engineering through valleys and mountains

The route has steady climbs through the valleys of the Ribble (Settle end) and Eden (Carlisle end) with a ten-mile mountain section which is almost level. All of this is over 1,100 ft above sea level (ASL). It is a masterpiece of engineering.

The River Ribble descends from over 900 feet close to Ribblehead to just over 400 Feet (ASL) at Settle Junction. In the Eden Valley from Hell Beck Gill, at over 1,100 feet, the river descends into the River Eden, which by Appleby is 400 feet ASL and under 100 by the time it reaches Carlisle.

From Settle Junction the railway climbs steadily for 6 miles to Helwith Bridge where there is an easing of the gradient. Ribblehead is just over 1,000 ft and the viaduct starts at 1,050 feet. Blea Moor tunnel (just under 15 miles from Settle Junction) is over 1,100 ft high with a high point of 1,151 ft.

Lofty viaducts and deep tunnels

Here, with few undulations, the railway remains for 10 miles in excess of 1,100 ft. The ten mile stretch from Blea Moor to Ais Gill has the railway clinging to the side of mountains, going over lofty viaducts or via deep tunnels.

There are, in fact, over 3.25 miles of tunnel. Blea Moor is 2,629 yards and Rise Hill 1,212 yards long. Two Stations, Dent and Hawes Junction (later Garsdale), are above 1,100 feet.

The valley floor is best shown at Dent/Lea Yeat nearly 400 ft below the railway. After Ais Gill the descent is to Appleby at 500 ft and later to Carlisle at 100 ft. After Lazonby the railway has to climb further away from the valley bottom to negotiate the Eden Gorge.

Local traffic on the route was not totally forgotten. Midland Railway built 19 stations, whilst the ascent from Carlisle to the summit was delayed to serve villages in the Eden Valley. The 40-mile stretch from Settle to Appleby is one of the most sparsely populated regions in England.

Rare visual unity for station design

It is not the purpose of this case study to describe in detail how the line was built. Others have done this too well. However, Jenkinson notes that the Midland Railway - using what might be called "Derby Gothic" for their station design - created a visual unity rare, if not unique, in the railways of Britain.

Commencement of goods and passenger traffic between mid-1875 and mid-1876

As it was, goods traffic commenced on 2nd August 1875 with passenger services commencing on 1st May 1876. Kenneth Duffin has put much flesh on the bones of earlier accounts and his chronology carries weight.

It is also worth noting that on 19th June 1876 the Rev E.H. Woodall of Settle wrote to the Midland Railway suggesting that the name of Batty Green station be changed to Ribblehead. This suggestion was adopted.

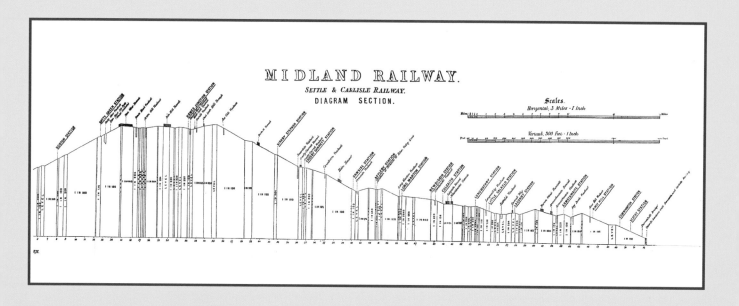

Making the Railway Work

Now a route to Scotland for the Midland - but longer than others

For the Midland Railway Company there was now a route to Scotland. However, the journey took longer than other routes. The route was 2 miles longer than via Ingleton and the journey from London to Edinburgh took 10 and a half hours. The LNWR route was 10 hours 10 minutes, whilst the East Coast route took 9 and a half hours.

Speed, comfort or punctuality

Baughan points out that the Midland faced a dilemma. This was whether to run non-stop through some of its lucrative territory and to beat the West Coast times, or to obtain more profit by calling at all major stations and offering superior standards of comfort and punctuality. For the first

20 years, the Midland pursued this latter option. Jenkinson also puts much flesh on the bones in respect of passenger and livestock traffic.

Pullman carriages introduced

To help on the passenger side, Allport came up with two ideas. It started with the introduction of Pullman Carriages. Later Midland came up with a high quality distinctive carriage for the Midlands - London - Scotland traffic as well as to Manchester.

Abolishing 3rd class coaches

The other change was effectively to abolish 3rd class coaches, which was completed in January 1875 when Midland abolished 2nd class travel. They broke up the wooden old third class carriages, replacing them with new carriages and upholstered seats. Thus, as others followed suit, the country had an anomaly of 1st and 3rd class travel until the mid-1950s.

CHAPTER 2 PART 2
Analysing the Decisions
1850-1880

Parliament and the Railways – an overview

Just a political game?

At first sight it may seem obvious that the most useful model to use to understand why certain decisions were taken is to see it as a *political game* between Parliament and the Railway Companies. However, that will only take us so far.

The railway companies were keen to get monopolies of traffic in their area. Parliament was concerned about monopolies and cartels and, as we have seen with the 1844 Railway Act, wished to give itself the option of nationalising some railway companies if necessary.

Failure to see the downside of competition

This Parliamentary opposition to "Railway Monopoly" helps explain why we are where we are now. Union of 'end on' was tolerated, but if parallel competitors wanted to unite it was considered unnatural. Parliament failed to see the downside of competition.

Rational actors

However, this is too simplistic. It had become obvious after a few years that the railway was to stay for a long time. Incidents and accidents happened and Parliament's approach to regulation, as exemplified in the 1844 Railway Acts, can be considered that of a *rational actor*.

In the same way, a lot of MPs (though not all) would have wanted railways to serve their areas. Thus, both Parliament and Railways at times were acting as *rational beings*.

Railway authorisations and Acts

There were over 100 railway authorisations. The number of Acts was much higher - up to 800 as companies had to go back to Parliament to request extension of time or for some modification to the route. The Midland Railway Company did this five times in respect of this line. However, as more Bills came forward, Parliament and the Civil Service would have wanted to address these in a

structured format that made sense not only to the House of Commons but also to the House of Lords - bearing in mind that more Prime Ministers sat in the House of Lords than in the Commons.

Here the *organisational process model* helps shed light on the decisions that were taken. What we see in the account by Duffin is clearly how the Parliamentary timetable affected decision making. Both the main Bill - 1865 - and the Abandonment Bill 1868 had to be submitted by 30th November of the previous year in accord with the start of the Parliamentary timetable.

We also realise that the authority to purchase the land lasted three years. Can we surmise what might have happened if Royal Assent from Queen Victoria had come three weeks earlier? Would Craske Roper have had time to complete the land purchase? Here the intervention of the solicitors in the summer of 1868 assumes a new importance.

The Midland Railway Company – distinction between Board and shareholders

It is at this stage perhaps helpful to make a distinction between the Board of the company and its shareholders. Quite often it is assumed that they had a single unity. In the Midland case, this could not really be further from the truth.

Rowdy scenes and manipulation of meetings

The shareholders met twice a year. Peter Baughan makes clear they were not sleeping partners, and the Board quite often had to deal with rowdy scenes and accusations of manipulation of meetings.

After the initial Bill had been passed (and in the light of Overend and Gurney), we see a lot of shareholder activity. At one stage a group of shareholders engaged a solicitor, Mr William Sale from Manchester, to petition LNWR behind the backs of the Midland Board to reach agreement. His proposal that the President of the Board of Trade should arbitrate in the dispute was ridiculed by the Midland Board.

In this area the Board and shareholders were both involved in *political manoeuvring* but at the same time the *organisational process model* is relevant, as without shareholder approval the Board could not proceed.

Approach to Parliament to build a railway

It could well be that the decision by LNWR not to allow Carlisle Station to be included in the proposed deal with the Midland Railway was the straw that broke the camel's back for James Allport and the Midland Railway Board.

LNWR were almost certainly trying to gain advantage over the Midland Railway and were playing *a political game*. It is a moot point as to whether or not LNWR wanted to break the deal or get themselves a better bargain.

In a bit of a sandwich, with a typically Midland solution

Some commentators have suggested that Allport acted in a "fit of pique", or alternatively, as a serious double bluff.

Yet the Midland, sandwiched between the West and East Coast Lines, needed to get decent access to Scotland. Jenkinson goes further: "…..the Midland was faced with the prospect of degenerating into a minor provincial railway unless it could develop fresh outlets." As such, the route was a typically Midland solution to its particular issues.

It can be explained as *a rational act and a political game.* However, the timetable set out by Duffin in relation to the North of England Union Railway, with the Midland taking over the Bill at the end of March 1865 and killing it on 29th June, actually pre-dates the authority given in early August for Crossley to survey the line - possibly even before Allport and Crossley did their initial walk. This suggests a *highly structured and rational approach* rather than an angry gesture.

Moreover, the Midland Board would have insisted on carrying out due diligence on the project. It was not in their interest to upset their shareholders or Parliament.

So Allport and Crossley would have done their initial walk before the 2nd August meeting. At that meeting the Board would have had to be convinced that further surveying work was appropriate - though not in the detail that Sharland eventually collected.

Who knew what about whom?

We now know that it must have been in August 1865 that Charles Stanley Sharland carried out his famous preliminary survey. Was it fortuitous that Allport and Crossley just happened to come across Mr Sharland at the Maryport and Carlisle Railway or was Crossley already aware of him?

It is difficult to believe that Allport and Crossley went to the August Board meeting without knowing who was going to carry out the survey for the line. Sharland, who had left the Maryport and Carlisle Railway, presumably to work on bigger projects, might have made a direct approach to Crossley. Alternatively, Allport and Crossley may have met him on their own initial survey.

Very clear about what was needed for a green light

Allport would also have been very clear about the processes he had to follow to get the green light from his Board, and to get his Bill presented to Parliament. The requirements of Parliament in terms of a detailed bill would also have been relevant. Allport would have assembled a team around him, as getting a bill to Parliament was not a three-person job. The *organisational process model* helps here. The timetable and range of skills necessary were highly significant.

Indeed, had the Parliamentary timetable allowed more flexibility, it is doubtful if the line would have been built with Overend and Gurney just around the corner.

Within Parliament there would have been *political* action. LNWR opposed the line and would have aimed to get MPs on their side. Caledonian would have done the same.

Support came from North British and Glasgow and South Western and Lancashire & Yorkshire. In the immediate locality those supporters of a line to Hawes would have supported the proposal together with advocates of links with the Eden Valley villages. Appleby, as a significant market town, was also strongly in support.

Playing a rational game

The Midland Railway company made certain concessions in this respect in what can be described as both *rational and political*.

The Bill passed the Commons and Lords in June 1866 - just one month after the collapse of Overend Gurney. The House of Lords agreed the bill on 26th June. Royal Assent came on 16th July.

1866-1869 - The Missing Years – or Ducks on Water - Overend and Gurney and North British

Turmoil beneath the surface

We know that in September 1866 John Crossley was instructed to begin staking out the line. On the surface not a lot was happening. Looking under the water there was turmoil.

Overend and Gurney was liquidated in June 1866. In September 1866 the whole Board of **North British** - a key ally in Scotland - resigned for financial malpractice.

Shockwaves through investor and railway communities

These two events would have sent shockwaves through the investor and railway communities. It is no small wonder that Crossley's work got nowhere.

North British could not contribute at all and were focused on seeing whether or not they could survive as an independent entity. Neither is it surprising that in Scotland the Caledonian Railway and Glasgow and South Western Railway started to talk to each other. Caledonian would have had to assess its role in the light of the Act and the North British problem and it was understandable that the two companies should talk.

Opening up communication channels

It is also inconceivable that Midland and LNWR did not open up communication channels. In due course, the Midland resolved its differences with Glasgow and South Western. All this makes the actions of five key individuals - Hutchinson, Price, Allport and Moon and Cawkwell - much more understandable, and probably *very rational decisions* at the time.

Indeed, had Hutchinson, Price and Allport decided in 1866 to proceed immediately with the line, they would have been judged by contemporaries and history as reckless and foolish.

Approach to Parliament 1869

Differences resolved

The outcome of this was that by November 1868 Midland and LNWR had resolved their differences. The Midland and LNWR presented their Abandonment Bill by 30th November 1868. The House of Commons Committee started its hearing on Thursday April 8th 1869. Six working days later the Bill was dead. Thanks to Peter Baughan, we can understand what happened. Three Railway companies were going to benefit

with better access to Scotland from England. None of these companies would have had to spend a penny to get the line open. They were Glasgow and South Western, North British and Lancashire and Yorkshire.

Their view seems to have been that the Midland Railway had used them as a bargaining tool in their discussions with LNWR. There was telling evidence from Lancashire and Yorkshire and North British regarding this.

The Wharncliffe intervention

The intervention by Lord Wharncliffe is interesting. He was heavily involved in the Manchester, Sheffield and Lincolnshire Railway (MSLR) and had been party to the withdrawal of the North of England Union Railway plan for a railway, once the Midland Railway had declared their hand. Interestingly, James Allport had been employed by MSLR for a three year period from 1850.

The link that Lord Wharncliffe had with Allport may have gone back some time – even to the Euston Square Confederacy that Gladstone helped break up in 1851. This might well have eased discussion over the NEUR plan. He might well have felt that Midland/Allport were not being entirely straight.

Other key players on the scene

Other key individuals, if only behind the scenes, were Sir James Lumsden, Lord Provost of Glasgow 1866-1869, Director of GSW from 1849 and Chairman from 1870-1879; from Northern British the Marquess of Tweeddale - Liberal MP for Taunton; and from Lord William Hay, who had led the rescue of North British in 1866. LYR tended to rely on their Counsel, Mr Pope, who from all accounts was impressive, and practical details from engineers and managers on the spot.

Early on it became clear that the fear in Scotland was that LNWR and Caledonian would prevent other companies from using Carlisle, whilst an admission had come that the Midland might need not actually run anything north of Ingleton to benefit from the deal.

Midland proposal thrown out by Parliament

The position of nearly every landowner had become clear, with 1,600 signing a petition. It did not need to be presented - but its influence would have been substantial. Parliament threw out the Midland proposal on 16th April 1869.

The *political process model* helps here - perhaps particularly with the Midland and LNWR - but the decision by other groups to oppose the Abandonment Bill can also be categorised as that of highly *rational actors.*

CHAPTER 3 PART 1
National and Local Narrative 1880-1948
Consolidation and Nationalisation

National Scene 1880 - 1923

Uncoordinated approach

The railways continued but in uncoordinated ways. This was in stark contrast to the situation in France, Germany or Belgium. In the UK there was no route master plan and route selection was left entirely to railway companies.

Preparing to take control during wartime

In 1871, under Gladstone's premiership, Parliament had passed an Act that allowed for sequestration of railways at time of war. This was activated prior to the First World War as the government took powers to take control of management, with a Railway Executive committee under the control of the War Office.

The government took power to limit profits to 1913 levels but paid not a penny for the assets. In addition, the government froze railway charges, whilst all war materials and personnel were carried free. This was in sharp contrast to industry, shipping and road transport. Railway costs were increased by industrial inflation, which left receipts well behind real costs.

Post-war developments and the creation of the Big Four

In 1919, the Ministry of Transport was formed with powers to nationalise railway management. Following problems in the coal industry, a Railway Act of 1921 amalgamated 130 railway companies into four. It came into effect on 1st January 1923.

The grouping of four companies - London Midland Scottish Railway, Great Western Railway, Southern Railway and London and North Eastern Railway - had been mooted 70 years earlier. However, the main reason for this action was to prevent bankruptcy of smaller railway companies whose finances were undermined by the war. It was felt that the "Big Four" could survive - as indeed they did. Full nationalisation had been on the table for discussion but was not the chosen option.

Road transport industry

Meanwhile, the infant road transport industry went into overdrive, powered by ex-military vehicles sold at knock down prices, available on HP. The War Office sold 80,000 and the US Army 9,000. Railway staff could only work an 8-hour day. Road hauliers had no such restrictions. For years hauliers paid little or nothing towards road costs. They could expand at will - the railways needed an Act of Parliament.

Oil-fired steam engines

Some experiments took place just after the war to save coal by using an oil tank on top of the coal tender and then injecting oil into the firebox. This was also tried in 1947.

Locally 1880 - 1923

Fast service to Scotland v Regional and local demands

Peter Baughan points out that the Midland faced a dilemma. This was whether to run non-stop through some of its lucrative territory and to beat the West Coast times, or to obtain more profit by calling at all major stations and offering superior standards in comfort and punctuality. For the first 20 years, the Midland pursued this latter option. Jenkinson makes clear that there was an obligation on the Midland to provide a Wensleydale Service after the NEUR buy-out.

Hamilton Ellis in *The Midland Railway* describes the 1870/80s as part of the Midland Railway Renaissance. Yet by 1900 he was describing troubled years before moving on to the Final Years up to 1923. Peter Baughan, too, describes the period 1884-80 as one of expansion, whilst 1891-1899 is a time of endeavour.

There are two really good sources of information. The first is Peter Baughan - the other is David Jenkinson. Both give examples of express train traffic. Jenkinson has analysed in depth the local passenger information. His analysis covers

1876-1963. However, the period 1923-53 is missing, whilst there is only part data for 1954-58.

The bottom line is that the East Coast and West Coast Lines made it difficult for the Midland to compete. With typical commercial sense the Midland opted for a three part solution: express trains to Scotland, a regional service and a specific service - both passengers and freight - to the local community.

Jenkinson makes the point "that the Settle and Carlisle Railway was built with very little *genuine* thought for the local community" despite Midland Railway protestations to the contrary. Yet there is significant evidence that this is what it had done.

Livestock

Jenkinson has also analysed movements in some detail. From about 6,000 truckloads in 1876-1885 the figure had risen by 1916-22 to nearly 10,000. Clearly, farmers made considerable use of the line. Jenkinson goes so far to assert that many current farmers would have had no farm to run had it not been for the Settle-Carlisle Line. From 1924 onwards the use fell substantially with the introduction of road transport.

Other freight

Other freight and mineral information is also available from Jenkinson. It is worth noting that Appleby and Kirkby Stephen were both served by other railways. As such, their figures are lower than anticipated. The freight figures for Lazonby are higher than anticipated. This is because of lots of minerals from Long Meg and larger amounts of livestock traffic.

Quarrying

Mark Rand in *Hopes for New Quarry Traffic* draws attention to the significant quarrying that took place on the stretch between Settle and Ribblehead, either for limestone, the processing of lime or stone per se. Extensive facilities were constructed at Stainforth, Helwith Bridge, Horton-in-Ribblesdale and Ribblehead. Some of the companies involved were Settle Limes, Helwith Bridge Granite Company, Ribblesdale Lime Company and Delaney's.

Commuter traffic

The line was not really originally conceived for commuter traffic. But as Baughan points out, the focus did change. Jenkinson illustrates that there was some commuter traffic, though this was really at the Carlisle end of the line. 1920 was the peak year for passenger traffic.

Express traffic

It can be said that the Anglo-Scottish traffic was a success. It was clearly the most scenic and comfortable route. However, the distance to Glasgow was 424 miles against 401 by the West Coast. The trip to Edinburgh Waverley was 407 miles compared with 393 along the East Coast.

Three serious accidents

There were three serious accidents. The first in 1910 on Christmas Eve at Hawes Junction saw 24 dead and 17 injured. It was the practice on the tough climb from Kirkby Stephen to Ais Gill to have a pilot train on most south bound trains from Carlisle. The engine would have its pilot uncoupled at Ais Gill and put into a lay-by siding. The pilot engine then followed the express to Hawes Junction to be turned on the turntable ready for return to Carlisle.

Two light engines were ambling back to Carlisle and were overtaken by the St Pancras-Glasgow sleeper and a terrible train fire ensued. The principal factor was human error, but it was also related to the Midland policy of using lighter engines. Baughan attributes responsibility to the Midland Railway, as a record of poor punctuality with erratic working of trains conflicted with the priorities of safety and signalling. This was also the case in 1913 at Ais Gill when 16 people died with 38 injured on 2nd September.

The cause of the third accident at Little Salkeld in 1918 on 19th January, when 7 people died, was a landslip.

World War 1

During the First World War the line played its part. In the early years it was involved heavily with troop movements but later the focus was on war materials. In early 1917 rolling stock and locomotives were moved to France and cuts were made to the service.

Nationally 1923 – 1948: Midland Railway - LMS - Nationalisation

Grouping of four companies

The grouping of four companies - London Midland & Scottish, Great Western Railway, Southern Railway and London and North Eastern Railway - led to some serious rationalisation. LMS, for example, inherited 10,316 steam locomotives made from 393 different specifications. However, the period 1923-39 saw significant investment into railway stock, locomotives, coaches and wagons.

Competition on speed

The four companies, though not in direct competition, nevertheless competed particularly on speed. Terms like "Flying Scotsman", "The Royal Scot", the "Coronation Scot" and "Cheltenham Flyer" have entered the vocabulary. Locomotives such as "Mallard", "Sir Nigel Gresley", "Silver Fox" and "Princess Margaret Rose" are just a few examples. It took the Big Four about 10 years to recover from their Herculean efforts during the war.

Investment in new stock and electrification

The serious investment into new stock was matched in the South of England by the massive electrification programme carried out by the Southern Railway. LMS and LNER also had some electrification programmes in Tyneside, Manchester and Merseyside. However, dozens of smaller uneconomic branch lines were closed - especially in Scotland and Northern England - their needs best met by road links.

Common carrier policy

When railway mania was at its height, Parliament had introduced a "Common Carrier" policy whereby anything had to be taken at a specific rate. The policy made sense at a time of monopoly, as it stopped the railways from "cherry picking" what goods they would carry. A parallel still exists with the Royal Mail being required to deliver each day to every location in the country.

Problems caused by growth of motor car and road transport

By the mid-late 1920s, with the growth of the motor car and road transport, it was causing significant problems for the railway companies as they had to carry freight at a loss. At that stage railway companies felt that half their income needed to come from freight. Remember that the track for cars and lorries was paid for by the local councils, whereas the railways had to look after their own lines, and many of the lorries had almost been gifted to the road haulage industry after the end of the war.

It was hoped that a 1931 Royal Commission on Road and Rail Transport would address this. It did not - at least not satisfactorily. Two years later a report by Arthur Salter made more sense. The remit was to consider the perception that safety, pricing and operating regulations placed the railways at an unfair disadvantage when compared with the road haulage industry.

The Minister of Transport, Oliver Stanley, lifted some restrictions on the railways and imposed certain conditions on the road haulage industry. Neville Chamberlain as Chancellor made the road industry pay full road fund costs but the railway common carrier obligation continued until 1957.

A key proposal was that the Treasury would make motor vehicles solely responsible for road costs and levy charges on motorised traffic rather than by funding via local government or penalising the railways. It recognised that road vehicles had been *"using the common highway for private profit, while endangering public safety, amenity and capital."*

Railways run a 'Square Deal' campaign that falls on deaf ears

The centralised funding of roads that came with the Trunk Roads Act 1936 heralded a new era. Indeed, the legacy left by the Salter Report can be compared with that of the Education Secretary, Richard Butler, with his 1944 Education Act. In 1938, the Railway Companies ran a "Square Deal Campaign" which asked for either equal commercial freedom or equal regulation of road transport. Released government files suggest that the Government wasn't going to accede to this request.

Railway network reduced between the wars

At the start of the First World War the network was 23,440 miles of track. By 1939 some 1,300 miles of track had been closed.

Different treatment of rail and road during wartime 1939-1945

The railways were again sequestered - unlike other transport or industry - and a lower profit limit imposed. Initially the government allowed wartime prices to rise to meet costs - subject to a tribunal - but later Churchill froze rail fares and freight fares for the duration. Other industries were allowed to raise prices to match cost increases under the Prices of Goods Act 1939.

In addition, the government imposed unique discounts on all war traffic. This did not apply to road traffic. By the end of the war industrial-fuelled inflation had opened up a huge gap between costs and income. The railways played a significant role during the Second World War. According to **Peter Hennessy** in *Never Again-Britain 1945-51*, the change on the railways was significant. Between the German invasion of Poland in 1939 and the Japanese surrender in 1945:

- Rail merchandise went up by 77%
- Mineral traffic rose by 35%
- Coal deliveries increased 9%
- Passenger numbers doubled

There was no proportionate increase in manpower and by 1942 locomotives were scarce. By 1944-45 they were teetering on the verge of collapse. Railway stock maintenance had fallen way below peace time standards, whilst little track maintenance had been carried out.

Wartime policies lead to insolvency

The approach adopted by the wartime government was forcing companies into insolvency. When BR started, it did so with 1941 prices and 1948 costs.

Post-war battle between the companies and the government

After the war a Labour Government held power. They believed that nationalisation would benefit the industry. This is not the place to analyse what went on but there was a battle royal between the railway companies and the government. The companies claimed unfair terms, offered alternative plans and wanted arbitration. The government refused. Alfred Barnes, a Labour Co-op politician, was Minister of Transport from 1945-51.

Transport Act of 1947 leads to Commission and Executive

Through the Transport Act of 1947 the Government created the British Transport Commission and dictated the organisation of nationalised transport including the composition of the Railway Executive and the boundaries of the Regions. The British Transport Commission took over the role of Railway Boards and the Railway Executives assumed the role of General Managers. The Act also established *Transport Users Consultative Committees*. Their terms of reference were modified in 1962. Later we shall see the role they played.

The birth of BR and a strange inheritance

The first Chairman of the British Transport Commission was a retired Civil Servant Sir Cyril Hurcomb. His department had devised the unwieldy organisation. Sir John Elliott (a senior railway manager and from 1951-53 the Chairman of the Railway Executive) in "On and off the Rails" said: "The organisation was entirely the work of civil servants and bore every sign of bureaucracy" The Chairman of the Railway Executive came from Southern Railway. He was Sir Eustace Missenden. So BR was born inheriting, amongst other stock, 8,793 horses from privately owned railways!

Financial restrictions and other controls

Both the Labour and Conservative governments imposed restrictions on what could be spent. In 1947 the Railways wanted to build 3,070 coaches but were limited to 1,200. Other controls remained in force until 1955. BR was instructed not to undertake wartime arrears of track renewal, and policies were implemented which would have bankrupted anyone else. Railway fares were fixed for 12 years by a court of law. Thus Ministers criticised BR for not making a profit, yet their own legislation made this impossible.

Locally 1923 - 1948: LMS into a nationalised railway system

The Midland Railway was assimilated into the London, Midland and Scottish Railway. Initially the LMS Board was dominated by the Midland Railway. LNWR individuals become more influential later but, after William Stanier joined in 1932 from Great Western Railway, the company tried to put an end to the bickering.

Settle - Carlisle in the 1920-30s

For detail it is best to look to Peter Baughan. He believes that with the focus on the quicker route over Shap the Settle-Carlisle Line began a slow and almost inexorable decline. Looking at the story during the war and later, this statement may need some qualification.

One of the difficulties analysts have is that the LMS records from 1923-1946 cannot be traced. One source remembers reading about a proposal in the 1930s emanating from LMS to close the Settle-Carlisle Line. However, it never got as far as public discussion.

Settle-Carlisle in wartime

During the 2nd World War, the West Coast Main Line took most of the passenger traffic. The Settle-Carlisle Line focused on freight. Locomotives found themselves underpowered on the 'Long Drag' with speed limits of 40mph. Things improved in 1943-44 when the Ministry of Supply provided larger locomotives. The Blea Moor loops were put in during this period. On 1st February 1942 Scotby station closed to all traffic.

Winter of 1947 - heroic stories

From early February 1947 the line was held in an icy grip for 8 weeks, with drifts over 12 feet thick. There are heroic stories in respect of passengers, but also livestock. As soon as some movement could be obtained, a host of new 'stations' appeared to enable feed to be got to the trapped animals.

Nationalisation - early days and a positive story about responding to floods

There is one positive story with which to end. Soon after nationalisation in1948, the East Coast Main Line suffered protracted flooding in the Northumberland area. The speed and efficiency in which alternative routes were set up and damage repaired has been held by many as a testimony to a nationalised railway. As an aside, the diversions saw the Kings Cross -Edinburgh "Flying Scotsman" run over the Settle-Carlisle and Waverley Lines.

CHAPTER 3 PART 2
Analysing the Decisions
1880-1948

Principle of monopoly - and Victorian governments' efforts to minimise it

To understand how decision making was made, it needs to be recognised that railways had been built on the principle of a monopoly of mechanical transport. Successive Victorian governments had tried to ensure that there were no complete monopolies. Thus, there was duplication of services and uneconomic lines had been built by different companies.

In this way, we can understand that the Victorian view of democracy was that the rich were stopped from being too powerful.

Arrival of motor car changes the game

The arrival of the motor car changed the balance for ever and the way that parties acted has to be reassessed in that light. Up until the end of the 2nd World War much of the decision making may be characterised as that of *rational actors.* The Conservative opposition to full nationalisation in 1921 can be seen either as wholly *rational* in protecting private companies or as that of *political actors.*

Infighting and gamesmanship

The initial infighting in LMS is what one expects to happen when different organisations are merged and is clearly characterised as *political gamesmanship* hiding several *rational actions*. It took the arrival of William Stanier from GWR to get the Board to focus on future opportunities rather than past rivalries.

It can be assumed that the difficulties the Royal Commission found in 1931 around the Common Carrier policy reflected an inability to negotiate a way around different *political actors,* whilst the 1933 Salter Report - with specific proposals which were adopted - can be described as *rational common sense*, given the remit of his committee.

Taxation of road transport to help the railways seen as 'foolish'

However, not all saw it that way. A former Transport Minister, Herbert Morrison, claimed that "the weapon of taxation of road transport as a means of putting the railways right was a foolish and idiotic policy". One by-product was that heavier steam traction was driven off the road in favour of lighter lorries using imported oil for their combustion engines.

Chamberlain willing to upset the road hauliers

The changes were applauded by the railway, industry but castigated by road hauliers. Thus the report was an example of both *rational and political* decision making. Chamberlain's willingness to upset part of the road haulage lobby suggests an act that was *rational and political.*

The placing of the railways onto a single wartime footing can in itself be described as a *rational action* by government, but there was clearly disagreement about whether or not railway prices ought to be allowed to rise and in that sense it might be recognised as having *political overtones.*

Likewise post-war, the nationalisation of the railways can best be described as being of a *political nature* but, with the creation of the British Transport Commission, we see that the *organisational process model* will be one crucial tool in analysing further decision making.

CHAPTER 4 PART 1
National and Local Narrative 1948-1962
The Run Up to Dr Beeching

Nationalised railway until Dr Beeching

British Transport Commission (BTC): charged with providing an integrated system

The Commission came into being on 1st January 1948. Its brief was to "provide an efficient, adequate and properly integrated system of public inland transport for passengers and goods, excluding air".

Its quasi-federal structure was problematic. As we have seen, the Commission itself undertook the role previously done by railway boards. The Railway Executive acted as General Managers, and traded as British Railways.

The first Chairman of the Commission was Sir Cyril Hurcomb. He retired for pastures new in 1953, specifically as an ornithologist, becoming Chairman and then President of the Royal Society for the Protection of Birds. He was succeeded by General Sir Brian Robertson, Bt, 1953-61, who was in turn succeeded by Dr Richard Beeching.

Under Sir Brian Robertson, in December 1954 the BTC published its Plan for Modernisation. The Commission was abolished at the end of 1962. Its railway responsibilities went to the British Railways Board from 1st January 1963.

Railway Executive: reorganising railways into six regions

The Railway Executive was a product of a bureaucrat's mind. Its first Chairman was Sir Eustace Missenden, a railway manager from Southern Railway. The first priority was to repair the infrastructure, clear the backlog of maintenance and start to make good losses in locomotives and rolling stock. The railways were organised into six Regions: London Midland, Southern, Eastern, Western, North Eastern and Scottish, in general relating to the old Big Four areas with the exception of Scotland.

Sir Eustace retired in 1951, being succeeded by Sir John Elliott until 1953. Sir John's background was also with Southern Railway. The Conservative government abolished the Railway Executive in 1953.

The six area boards were given autonomy and responsibility for fares and told to seek the maximum charge, even though they were still theoretically accountable to the parent body. In 1958 the regions were given a more geographical re-alignment.

Plan for modernisation: and a dash of over-optimism

The Plan for Modernisation unveiled in December 1954 noted that there were 18,426 steam locos - just 1,000 fewer than in 1938. It wanted a big push towards electrification and dieselisation. It also foresaw large marshalling yards for freight, and hoped to reduce deficits quite quickly. This was almost certainly an optimistic assessment.

Rail Network 1949-1962: closure of over 3,000 miles of track

In 1949 the British Transport Commission created a "Branch Lines Committee" with a brief to close the least-used railway lines. By the end of 1962, 3,318 miles of track had been closed.

Conservative government

Seeking a profitability that did not come

Following their victory in the 1951 General Election, the Conservative government wanted a return to competition, commercial policy and administrative decentralisation. As much as anything they were determined that the network should be profitable. However, after 10 years this had not materialised. By 1960 the annual railway deficit was £60 million. Two years later it was £104 million. This was working out at £300,000 per day.

In 1956 a White Paper was produced on the funding and structure of the British Transport Commission. But by 1960 they considered it to be a failure. The Guilleband Committee recommended a wage increase for rail workers. The government response was to produce a White Paper planning an extensive re-organisation of railway administration, and the possible closure of uneconomic routes.

Introducing Ernest Marples MP and Dr Richard Beeching

We now need to understand a little more about Ernest Marples, MP and Dr Richard Beeching.

Ernest Marples

Alfred Ernest Marples was the key transport minister during this period. Marples had grown up in a Labour background and had jobs as a miner, postman, chef and accountant. He was invalided out of the Army in 1944 with the rank of captain and had by that time become a Conservative.

In 1945 he entered Parliament as MP for Wallasey. In 1951, prior to the election, he had come to the notice of Harold Macmillan with his support for a housing programme. Macmillan, as Secretary of State for Housing, appointed Ernest Marples to the lowest rung of the Ministerial ladder.

When Macmillan took over as Prime Minister after the Suez crisis, Marples was appointed Postmaster General. Here, he helped Macmillan introduce Premium Bonds, was involved with subscriber trunk dialling and the first postcodes used by Royal Mail. Later, as Transport Minister, in addition to his railways involvement, he was involved with parking meters, traffic wardens, yellow and double yellow lines, provisional driving licences and MOT tests for cars.

Conflict of interest

Marples had made money with a road construction company, Marples Ridgeway. On joining the government in 1951, he had resigned as MD of the company. However, he had held on to 80% of the firm's shares. On his appointment as Secretary of State for Transport on 14th October 1959, it was realised there was a conflict of interests. He was told to sell his shares.

By 1960 this had still not happened. In and around that time his former company was winning substantial contracts for flyovers at Hammersmith and Chiswick and the Hendon Urban Motorway. In the end he got rid of his shares to his wife.

No coincidence

History does not accept that this was a reasonable thing to do. There seems to be a general view that the relationship between Marples and Beeching was such that it was no coincidence that Dr Beeching closed railways whilst his boss's firm built new roads.

Marples as an individual was probably no saint. Later on he fled to Monaco to avoid possible prosecution for alleged tax fraud, it is claimed.

Dr Richard Beeching

Dr Richard Beeching had a distinguished record as a physicist and technical director working for ICI. He came to the attention of Ernest Marples and Harold Macmillan in an indirect way. Marples had decided that he needed to have a proper look at the financing of the British Transport Commission.

In 1960 an invitation was extended by the Prime Minister to Sir Ivan Stedeford to chair the Advisory Group on Transport. Sir Ivan had a record as a leading industrialist and philanthropist. Indeed, a hospital in India still bears his name. He had worked his way up and been Managing Director and Chairman of Tube Investments - a major British company.

In looking for members of the committee, Marples approached Sir Frank Smith, who had just retired from working as Richard Beeching's boss at ICI. Sir Frank declined but suggested Dr Beeching as a member.

A furious clash with Sir Ivan

Sir Ivan and Dr Beeching clashed furiously about suggestions that Dr Beeching was making to cut the railway network and wanting to lose up to a third of a million wagons. Sir Ivan presented his report but it was not published for many years.

In addition to Sir Ivan, there were five other members of his Committee. They were Richard Beeching, Henry Benson, (Partner in Cooper Brothers), David Serpell (Dept. of Transport), M Stevenson (Treasury) and C.F.Kearton (Joint Managing Director of Courtaulds).

Sir Ivan had called for an end to what he described as the railways' *public service* mentality, recommending that they be run on a profit making basis.

In March 1961, Marples announced that Dr Beeching was to be appointed as Chairman of the first British Railway Board, taking up duties on 1st June 1961 initially as Chairman of the British Transport Commission. His salary was the same as at ICI, namely £24,000 a year. This equates to £367,000 today.

Did he jump or was he pushed?

Dr Beeching was seconded to the government for a five year period. His first report, entitled "The Re-shaping of British Railways", came out on 27th March 1963. On 23rd December 1964 the Labour Minister of Transport, Tom Fraser, announced that Dr Beeching would return to ICI in June 1965 - one year earlier than originally planned.

It is a matter of dispute whether Dr Beeching was sacked. Frank Cousins, Labour Minister of Technology, says he was. Dr Beeching denied this.

Second report rejected by the government

On 16th February 1965 Beeching announced his second report on the development of major railway trunk routes calling for a trunk railway of only 3,000 miles with traffic being focused on nine major lines. This report was rejected by the Government.

Scapegoat or part of a wider conspiracy

It is not intended to explore this at any length. Some argue that his rail replacement services by bus were never a success, that he ignored economies that could have been made and simply got figures wrong.

He has also been accused of being part of - or a scapegoat for - a conspiracy against the railways involving politicians, civil servants and the road lobby.

For years there seems to have been a link between the Conservative party and the road lobby, but some also argue that the Labour Government bowed to its union friends who worked on the roads.

Others say that the Treasury was more influential in policy making than the road lobby and that Ministers should have been responsible for assessing the social case for lines and that economies had been tried and failed.

Locally 1948–1962: Nationalised railways until Dr Beeching

London Midland Region

After 1948, the Leeds-Settle-Carlisle Line passed into the London Midland Region of British Railways. However, Baughan writing in 1965 tells us that the line south of Skipton was in the North Eastern Region.

Positive initiatives

It is not intended here to list all of whatever new initiatives there were - but they existed for both freight and passenger services. More detail can be had from Peter Baughan.

The minerals saga

Jenkinson points out that purely local mineral traffic had declined from pre-war levels. Several stations had closed to mineral traffic in the 1950s and at the end of the period the only major locations were Horton, New Biggin and Lazonby with the Long Meg quarry.

In preparing his book - published in the early 1970s - Jenkinson contacted quarry owners with a battery of questions. The few areas with rail links were the gypsum and anhydrite quarries in the Eden Valley (Long Meg and New Biggin) and limestone quarries at Helwith Bridge, Horton and Ribblehead.

In most cases he found that the amount of minerals carried by rail had been decreasing for a long time and that the railway was then used because it was there - not because it was essential.

Winter 1962-63: beyond the call of duty

As in 1947 there was a severe winter, closing the line for five days. Once again, staff went well beyond the call of duty to look after passengers.

Station closures on Settle-Carlisle route

This period saw a number of closures. In 1952 Cotehill, Crosby Garrett and Ormside were closed to all traffic. In 1956 Cumwhinton went the same way. The line to Hawes was closed on 6th March 1959. Just off the line Bell Busk closed in May 1959.

More significantly, the Railway Executive had considered the merits of closing either the Settle-Carlisle Line or the Ingleton Branch Line. On grounds of public amenity, they closed Ingleton to general passenger traffic in February 1954. The exceptions were two public schools whose boarders were able to travel to and from school at the beginning and end of each term. In fact, there were six trains per year. The whole line was closed in early 1965.

Line closures adjacent to Settle-Carlisle Railway

This period saw the start of closure of lines that linked or touched the Settle-Carlisle Railway. In respect of North Eastern Railway the start was made in July 1960 with the closure of the Kirkby Stephen-Tebay Line, and by January 1963 the only relevant NER link was between Appleby East and Kirkby Stephen East.

Jenkinson wonders whether or not one of the first casualties, which was the old LYR passenger link from Blackburn to Hellifield in 1962, was related to old rivalries.

Accidents

There were four accidents worth noting. On 29th November 1948, a crane ran out of control at Griseburn. It ran for 23 miles - fortunately in the right direction - until stopping at Lazonby. One person died and two were injured. On 18th April 1952, an express derailed near Blea Moor. Twenty-nine people were injured, the cause being faulty engine maintenance.

On 21st January 1960 a Glasgow-St Pancras express experienced serious knocking noises. The driver checked at Garsdale but, in horrible conditions, he hoped he could get to Hellifield. Probably travelling too fast, his piston rod broke and the train crashed into a goods train at 01.48 hours, half a mile from Settle Station. Five people died whilst nine were injured.

1961 saw two accidents. On August 22nd two freight trains were involved in a derailment near Little Salkeld station, whilst on September 8th, close to Stainforth sidings, a freight train crew from Carlisle realised that the rear part of the train had broken away and that rear wagons on the main part had de-railed. One guard was injured. The cause in both cases was almost certainly faulty loading.

CHAPTER 4 PART 2
Analysing the Decisions 1948-1962

The Civil Service

A well-oiled, efficient machine?

It is here that we need to face up to two different hypotheses. The first, supported by the Civil Service (and probably no one else), is that the Civil Service is a well-oiled, highly efficient and impartial body of men (sic) giving truly sensible advice to their political masters and taking immediate steps to implement their masters' wishes, whilst at the same time protecting them from problems.

Where does Sir Humphrey come into it?

This Civil Service sees itself as clean, decent, honest and honourable. It is all these things. But that is not the whole picture. This is not the model made famous with Sir Humphrey Appleby in "Yes Minister". The strength of the series by Jonathan Lynn and Antony Jay lies in its closeness to reality. Peter Hennessy, the noted post war historian, is withering in his assessment. He clearly sides with Jay and Lynn.

The war time Civil Service had recruited widely from outside - men and women with practical skills. They departed quickly with the Civil Service not really wanting them.

Managing the status quo rather than modernising the British economy

The Civil Service was not in the business of modernising our economy - it was managing the status quo. Here, the post war contrast with France - c.f. Sir Edward Bridges, Head of the Civil Service and Guy Monnet in France, is astonishing. After the war (with the honourable exception of a young Sir Oliver Franks), the Civil Service reverted to a business-as-usual arrangement that had applied pre-war.

Peter Hennessy describes it thus: "They simply refused to face up to it - a classic example of the myopia that can befall a largely self-regulating profession."

Square peg in a round hole

Sir Cyril Hurcomb - a bureaucrat's bureaucrat - had created a board noted for its age, caution and drabness, whilst it is probably best to describe Sir Eustace Missenden (Chairman of the Railway Executive) as a square peg in a round hole. Never one to work overlong hours, he found the task of dealing with the egos of his colleagues too difficult. His fellow board members had been recruited from the Big Four railway companies. Not only did they have their own agendas - they clearly resented the fact that someone from Southern Railway had been recruited to do the job.

All of this suggests that the **_organisational process model_** will help a lot in understanding what happened.

Self-financing ambitions

The philosophy espoused by the Conservative Party post-1951 (and I suspect the Labour Party as well) was that the railways needed to be self-financing. This was at the heart of discussions for the following 40 years.

Jenkinson points out that there was a time when both rich and poor were dependent on public transport. Although this may be true for the period up to the late 1950s, it is not the case today outside of major conurbations like London.

There will always be people who are dependent on public transport. However, no transport operator can run profitably when serving a diminishing part of the community. We will be returning to this issue later.

Plan for modernisation

Behind the continent in use of diesel traction or electrification

In analysing the plan it needs to be understood that post-war Britain had not used diesel traction or electrification as much as continental railways. Some consider that this was due to Clement Attlee's attempts to protect the coal industry and the balance of payments. However, in the light of the coal shortages in the winter of 1947 and the use of oil fired locomotives, this may need to be re-assessed.

The call in the 1954 plan for marshalling yards was a big mistake. A host of diesel shunters were ordered, whilst at the time local rail freight traffic was falling. The plan also failed to see the potential growth of container traffic. The introduction of diesel traction did not go well. There were too many companies producing diesel locomotives. Some succeeded - others did not - and they were being replaced within 10 years.

The plan itself did not really challenge any pre-war practices - again like the Civil Service - not looking ahead.

By 1962 the plan for modernisation had been recognised as a failure. *It had led to significant mistrust within the Treasury of any future financial forecasting coming from British Rail managers.* As we will see, this had long term serious consequences for rail transport.

Marples legacy

Non-rail

Leaving aside the railway legacy of Ernest Marples, it is probably fair to reflect that many of his other initiatives were a product of their time and not related to any particular genius he had.

Premium Bonds were a Prime Ministerial initiative, though Marples was a great salesman, whilst Subscriber Trunk Dialling owed its position to technical developments. Marples' other initiatives - for example, yellow lines and MOTs - are really akin to Hore Belisha's introduction of the Belisha Beacon in the 1930s. Essentially any minister would have done the same. As such, they are probably *rational decisions* made possible by *organisational* developments.

Railways

This is not the place to analyse this too much. Doing something was *rational.* Doing what Marples did was highly *political* and, because he held conflicting personal interests, verged on the *criminal.*

Details of the Beeching legacy

It is not intended to explore this at any length. Some argue that his rail replacement services by bus were never a success, that he ignored economies that could have been made, and that he simply got figures wrong.

Civil Servants and Ministers of one mind

With the benefit of hindsight, it is possible to realise that in the early 1960s there was within the Civil Service a thinking that was identical to that of Ministers.

In the years running up to Tom Fraser's announcement, at the end of 1964, that Dr Beeching would return to ICI one year early, we can see that when Beeching pushed his agenda he would have found little opposition from within the Department of Transport.

Dr Beeching - an executive civil servant - was in a position to implement a radical agenda with total Civil Service and ministerial backing. This does not happen often. Indeed, the last time the Civil Service had experienced this would have been in wartime.

Verging on the fanatical

We shall see later how this was pursued with a thoroughness that at times verged on the fanatical. However, the context of losses of £300,000 per day does need to be recognised.

Obviously, in such a complex business, there were *rational decisions* made. Quite obviously, *organisational factors* came into play - not least in the consultative processes or a recognition that moving all freight onto one or two lines before electrification was not feasible. However, the decision making process was clearly influenced by *political factors* - not least the relationship that Beeching had with Marples.

CHAPTER 5 PART 1
National and Local Narrative
Closure Plans

Nationally – 1962-1989: Dr Beeching and beyond

Approach

So much happened during this period that it would fill a book to do justice to this. That is not the purpose of this case study, so the narrative will explore specific themes. For a fuller picture, go to Abbott and Whitehouse - *The Line that Refused to Die* or to James Towler - *The Battle for the Settle & Carlisle*.

Many individuals and organisations contributed to the eventual saving of the line and played significant and crucial roles. At one level, it is arguable that no individual references should be made. With certain organisations, this has not proved possible.

Beeching summary - many of his proposals inevitable, and economically justified

Dr Beeching argued that one third of route miles carried 1% of passengers. Of 18,000 coaches, 6,000 were used only 18 times per year. In addition, he argued that half the network carried 4% of passengers and 5% of freight.

This generated revenue of £20 million against costs of £40 million. The other half of the network made substantial profits. He specifically recommended that 2,363 (55%) stations should close whilst 6,000 (30%) miles of track should go.

Dr Beeching's 1965 report, arguing for a much reduced trunk network, was quickly rejected by the Labour Government. Whilst some rationalisation could make sense, it would seem to be impractical for all Birmingham to London traffic to go via New Street to Euston, or to undertake essential engineering work or electrification without alternative options.

Dialogue of the deaf - London beer

Looking back and assessing the impact of Dr Beeching, it is clear there were two schools of thought. It is almost as if there was a dialogue of the deaf, with neither side finding common ground. One example will suffice.

It comes from the transport of cask beer from breweries at Burton-on-Trent to the vaults of St Pancras Station, London. Here, much of the beer drunk by Londoners was moved on. When building St Pancras station, it was realised that a large underground vault could be used for commercial purposes.

The breweries at Burton on Trent had soft water and improved techniques and were able to produce a clear, stable brew very different from darker London stouts. A vast storage area was constructed to take three trains a day - more in October of each year. Soon after Dr Beeching took office, the traffic was stopped by BR, although the line remained open. The beer then went by road on the new motorways. For some, this was an example of political interference by Marples.

The counter argument had three elements to it:

● The great railway pioneers had made an assumption that half of their income needed to come from passenger traffic and half from freight

● Once the monopoly enjoyed by the railways had been broken, it was inevitable that over time significant amounts of freight would be lost to the roads

● Beeching did not want to repeat the mistakes of the Plan for Modernisation. He wanted bulk commodities on a regular basis. For example, coal, steel, iron ore, road stone, oil and petrol. Someone in BR determined that beer did not fit this criteria

In this way, it was difficult for those on either side of the debate to find ways to have constructive discussions on the basis of genuine goodwill.

Miles of track lost

We have seen how in the 13 years before Beeching, British Rail closed 3,000 miles of track. In the period 1963/1974, British Rail lost 4,066 miles of track.

Over the period from 1950-1973, 7,171 miles of track were closed. Of these, broadly 4,170 could be attributed to Conservative governments and 3,001 to two Labour Governments.

Thousands of passengers lost

In 1961, passenger number were 1,026 million. By 1969, passenger numbers were down to 805,000. Later years saw a climb back until now they have exceeded their earlier peak.

Government during this period

The Conservative Government that had initiated the Beeching Report remained in power until October 1964. A Labour Government was then in power until June 1970. The Conservatives were in power from 1970 until February 1974, when Labour took over again. The Conservative Party under Margaret Thatcher was in power from May 1979 until the end of the period under review.

Labour initiatives

The Labour Party carried on with the Beeching proposals even if in modified form. Barbara Castle took over from Tom Fraser as Transport Minister in December 1965 and in 1967 published a map, Network for Development, showing stabilisation of route miles at around 11,000.

Later, Barbara Castle gave her consent to the closure of the Waverley Line to Edinburgh. In 1968, she introduced Metropolitan Transport Authorities, of which four were up and running by early 1970.

Conservative initiatives

Within the early Heath government there was general acceptance that the railway network closure programme had reached its natural end. It is also worth noting that freight lines could be closed overnight with no discussion whatsoever.

The experience of BR under Mrs Thatcher was generally positive. A consensus exists that it was stronger in 1990 than in 1979.

Indeed, Mrs T. famously told Nicholas Ridley *"No, No, No, - Railway Privatisation will be the WATERLOO of this government."* when he suggested privatisation of BR. (See Chapter Notes).

Early into the Thatcher years we had the Serpell Report. David Serpell from the Department of Transport had been a member of the Stedeford Committee. He was asked to produce two reports addressing the decline in traffic. His first report came up with a number of options for Ministers. This in itself was unusual but it did not address the size of the rail network. Interestingly, he was not asked to look at this. No network changes resulted from his initial report. A second report followed in 1992 on the rail network.

Paul Channon's 'annus horribilis' - from King's Cross fire to Lockerie air disaster

Between November 1987 and January 1989 Paul Channon, Secretary of State for Transport from June 1987, suffered what someone on a higher pay grade later called "an annus horribilis".

On 18th November 1987, 31 people were killed in the Kings Cross Fire. Just over a year later, on 12th December 1988, 35 people were killed in the Clapham Junction Rail disaster.

Nine days later, on 21st December, 270 people died in the Lockerbie air disaster, and about three weeks later 41 people died when British Midland Flight 92 crashed onto the M1 at Kegworth whilst heading for East Midlands Airport.

Backroom boys in the Civil Service and their advisers

Treasury civil servants and a loss of confidence in BR management

We have already seen how Treasury civil servants lost confidence in BR managers. This was over the Plan for Modernisation with marshalling yards. A host of highly efficient yards were built, but were left idle with no work to do. Had that money been put into signalling, capacity would have increased, and revenue savings made.

Towards a more hands on approach

Putting aside any possible pro-road agenda that might have existed, Treasury civil servants were not going to be hoodwinked a second time. Almost certainly their mistrust moved them towards a more hands on approach with their colleagues in the Department of Transport.

Cooper Brothers

One name that crops up as being of importance is that of Cooper Brothers, a very significant audit and accounting firm used by British Rail and others. The firm had been founded in 1854 and built up a significant reputation.

In 1957, it became Cooper and Lybrand - but continued trading under the Cooper Brothers name in the UK for some years until it traded as Coopers and Lybrand. In 1998, it merged again to become PriceWaterhouseCoopers.

Focus on stemming the £300,000 a day loss

It needs to be recognised that Coopers would have been working to a client's brief (Treasury or Department of Transport), that focused on reducing losses of £300,000 per day. It is not clear whether the philosophy was imposed by Whitehall, or if they

adapted a formula used in advising other clients, and used it for Dr Beeching without the full implications being evident.

The Cooper Brothers system adopted by Beeching and BR and others ignored traffic that used the route as part of a journey to get from A to B and put all the costs of the line onto traffic just using - in this case - the 72 miles.

In ignoring income from other sources including branches, as well as ignoring any value that a route would have as a diversionary facility - in this case the West Coast Main Line - benefits to the whole tree were missed. As none of this income could be guaranteed, it is understandable why a different approach was used.

Treasury assessments and accounting methods

This is not the place to try to explore in depth different accounting techniques used in different countries. At that time, Treasury assessments of value for money took into account additional tax raised on petrol purchased by drivers. Rail passengers were not paying duty directly, and when passengers moved to car transport, tax revenues rose. It could justify a case study on its own.

British Rail management tactics and culture

Once Dr Beeching left, he was replaced by a series of knights. Stanley Raymond from 1965-67, Henry Johnson from 1967-71, Richard Marsh from 1971-76, Peter Parker from 1976-83 and Sir Robert Reid from 1983-90. He in turn was followed by Sir Bob Reid from 1990-95.

A careful consideration of the history of Dr Beeching indicates that senior railwaymen were initially horrified by, but later absorbed, the philosophy and the need for change. Railway officers who did not "read the script" included Gerry Fiennes and Ron Cotton. Gerry Fiennes saved the East Suffolk Line against the tenor of Beeching and got away with it, as did Ron Cotton (see later) with the Settle-Carlisle Line. These were exceptions.

Line closures rather than cost reductions and income generation

It can be seen with hindsight that the predominant focus of BR and its management was to make the necessary savings through line closures, rather than attempting to reduce costs or maximise income.

Interestingly, one moral of the whole Settle-Carlisle story is that they were not as tactically astute as they would have liked us to believe.

Cost exaggeration - revenue minimisation

A prime tool used by BR and civil servants was to maximise costs and to underplay the revenue received. This approach went on for over 30 years and was seen by those at the top as a legitimate approach. In the short time before Dr Beeching reported, many stations filled all vacancies.

In this way, the argument about line viability was skewed right from the start. The principal argument accepted for reducing running costs was line closure. This, of course, was nonsense. We shall see later how the Ribblehead Viaduct Saga fits into this category.

When it came to costs, the approach was similar. It started with a standard approach to move asset renewal dates until just after the scheduled closure. In this way a line could confidently be predicted to make a loss.

The hardship test prevails

BR made no allowance for costs that would remain even if line closure went ahead - e.g., upkeep of bridges. In the same way, when calculating revenue, Abbott and Whitehouse describe time and time again how BR used "regular passengers" as the norm. Here, the test that had to be applied to closure of a line was the "hardship test".

In this way, only those living in the area of the line, and using the line on a regular basis, counted. According to BR there were 43 regular passengers. For example, passenger income from someone going from Glasgow to St Pancras was ignored whilst holiday or youth hostelling income was taken out of the equation. This accreditation of fares to the purchase station only was quite deliberate.

Land disposal

Beeching made no reference to land disposal. British Rail disposed of land that was no longer needed. In the USA closed track beds were retained by the Rail Bank Scheme. This was not considered desirable (or even feasible in the UK with a much smaller land mass) and a policy evolved of building houses on removed tracks. It was said that this was to prevent lines re-opening.

Transport Users Consultative Committees (TUCCs)

Any closure proposal had to go before a TUCC. Under TUCC rules, it was forbidden to cross-examine BR on its own figures. People questioning this were thrown out of meetings.

A similar argument applied with roads, as no one could question the Ministry of Transport estimates for new roads. This continued until the Winchester by-pass scheme, when protesters realised that if they rioted at meetings and stopped them from legally finishing, the process had to continue on and on. Eventually, the bureaucrats backed down.

The 'bustitution' policy - a false argument that persisted until 1990

A key element from the early days of Beeching until 1990, was the argument put forward of accommodating passengers on buses. Not only was this much slower but there was never any agreement that services would continue for more than, say, three years. It was really a false argument but civil servants kept putting it forward as a logical policy.

Classic closure tactics - closure by stealth

It is worth quoting from the Craven Herald article of 25th April 2009, which celebrated the reprieve after 20 years.

"A combination of strange pricing policies, cancelled trains, the neglect of maintenance over a period of years and warnings of how few passengers were using the line were well-known as measures adopted by British Rail in the run-up to any official statement".

Ironically, Ron Cotton, also used stealth tactics to help keep the line open

Settle-Carlisle and West Coast Main Line

Some evidence exists that there were three way discussions between BR, the Department of Transport and the Treasury about electrification. The Treasury line was first that electrification would go as far as Crewe. After pressure from BR and the Department of Transport, this was extended to Preston. However, BR still wanted electrification to Glasgow and Edinburgh via Carstairs.

The Treasury said *yes if BR agreed to close the Settle-Carlisle Line.* Indeed, this is illustrated in an article in the April 2014 "Rail" Magazine commemorating 25 years since reprieve.

Ron Herbert, a signalling engineer, explained in depth how he was instructed to get freight off the Settle-Carlisle Railway. But, in the end, this proved impossible.

Diversionary route for West Coast Main Line

Dr Beeching and BR seem not to have evaluated the significance of the Settle-Carlisle Line as a diversionary route for the West Coast Main Line. This is a general criticism that can be made against the Beeching proposals.

Freight: Settle-Carlisle and West Coast Main Line - 20 year wait

Dr Beeching intimated in 1963 that the Settle-Carlisle Line should close. It was 20 years later in December 1983 that BR issued its first formal closure notice.

We need to try and understand why this was. In 1970, when Lt Col McNaughton reported on the 1968 Horton goods accident, he had been told *"this route is planned for closure in the next few years"*.

I think it fair to say that this was not because of a massive rear-guard action within BR against line closure. It is almost certainly due to a practical problem which civil servants in the Department of Transport and the Treasury eventually recognised and understood.

It relates to "unfitted freight". Back in mid-Victorian times, after some appalling accidents, Government legislation enforced continuous brakes on passenger services. Companies were allowed to choose air brakes or vacuum brakes. Air brakes were better but more expensive than vacuum brakes. The railway companies tended to opt for vacuum brakes. However, this legislation *did not apply to freight.* Until we caught up with the rest of the world in the 1980s and used only air-braked freight trains, there were three types of goods trains.

Unfitted - Loose coupled

These trains had steam brakes on the loco and hand brakes on the tender. The hand brake in the guard's van could be used in motion to control trains. The handbrakes on the wagons were essentially "parking" brakes. It took great skill to operate. If the guard braked too soon, the train would break in half, and if the driver did the same, the wagons would pile up.

The system was cheap and allowed lower powered locos to start heavier trains. Those of an older generation will recall times when it took a goods train quite a while to get moving forward at the rear.

Semi-fitted

Here, the loco had steam and vacuum brakes and a hand brake on the tender. A proportion of the train next to the engine had wagons tightly coupled with continuous vacuum brakes, with a further portion loosely coupled with hand brakes. The vacuum braked part near the engine was called the fitted head and the bigger the head the better the speed - worked out precisely by formula.

Fully-fitted

Here, the train was tightly coupled with vacuum brakes and the only restrictions on speed compared to a passenger train were vehicle stability and train weight.

The Settle-Carlisle Line was used by unfitted freight, which could not realistically use the West Coast Main Line because of speed and volume restrictions. When Sir Peter Parker retired in 1983, he was replaced by Sir Robert Reid. He created five clear divisions in BR and made them financially autonomous. Once this happened, BR quickly fitted air brakes to all freight.

Local Narrative 1962-1990

10-year saga

Some details of what happened (drawn from Abbott and Whitehouse) are outlined in a thematic basis in Appendix 2. After some brief background information, I want to explore a limited number of themes.

Beeching summary

When Dr Beeching published his report, he argued that only Appleby and Settle were running at a profit. He proposed withdrawal of passenger services, leading to eventual closure of the line. His report showed that in respect of passengers south of Appleby, the number was between 10,000-50,000 per week. North of Appleby the figures were 5,000-10,000 per week.

In terms of freight and materials, approximately 100,000 tons per week were being carried over the Settle-Carlisle Line as opposed to half of that over the Shap route.

He intended to close the central mountain section, which included all the major civil engineering (tunnels and viaducts etc.), but to retain single track "twigs" at each end to retain valuable freight traffic, particularly from Settle Junction to Ribblehead. One can understand the logic of this approach without having to agree with it.

Accidents

An accident occurred on 30th October 1968 at 00.16 hours, at Selside near Horton-in-Ribblesdale. Two goods trains collided. A train from Preston to Carlisle ran into the back of a stationary train (Warrington to Carlisle) at 30 mph. The second train was waiting for clearance to move to Blea Moor. Two people were injured.

The damage resulted in 45 passenger trains and 125 freight trains being diverted. The cause of the accident was that the driver of the goods train was asleep. Poor cab ventilation was a factor. Lt Col McNaughton, in his report in 1970 (available at 1s 9d or 9p), said that had British Rail employed its AWS system the accident would have been averted.

It was low down on BR's list of priorities and was expensive to install. As the route was planned for closure in the next few years, it made no economic sense to proceed.

British Rail manoeuvres towards closure

The general approach by British Rail towards rail closures has already been described and can equally be related to the Settle-Carlisle Line.

Yet in the space of 18 months, BR had made three crucial decisions on the closure all of which were to backfire on them. The first was an attempt to persuade Cumbria County Council to drop opposition to the line closure plan. The second related to the Ribblehead Viaduct. The third was the appointment of the Project Manager to close the line.

Councils - and an attempt to put pressure on Cumbrian politicians

There were four county councils potentially involved. In the early years North Yorkshire CC was reluctant to get involved, not seeing the Settle-Carlisle Line as one of their priorities. This position changed over time. The three others were Cumbria, Lancashire and West Yorkshire. Of course, there were many other district councils as well as the Yorkshire Dales National Park Authority.

In May 2014, Peter Robinson, who earlier in his career had been an officer with Cumbria County Council, recounted how on 28th May 1980 the Cumbria Council Leader, Councillor Bill Cameron, and others were taken on a BR trip around the Cumbrian Coast.

An offer was made by a BR Divisional Manager of a £7 million investment in the Cumbrian Coast Line as long as Cumbria CC did not object to BR proposals to close the Settle-Carlisle Line. This was immediately rejected and Cumbria CC took on an ever higher profile in the campaign against closure. Sadly, Peter Robinson died in August 2014 aged 74. (See Chapter notes)

Ribblehead Viaduct - overblown repair estimates in an attempt to force closure

It was in the first half of 1981 that a campaign was started by BR managers in the railway and local media to close the Ribblehead Viaduct.

It is thought that the BR Chairman, Sir Peter Parker, was kept in the dark about this. Using estimates that were later put to shame, BR indicated that the viaduct would cost £10 million to repair and that over 10 years £600,000 had been spent, leaving it in a worse state than when they started. The blame was put on the original construction. We now know this to be false and the viaduct was repaired for £2.5 million.

It was a former BR engineer, Chris Wallis (eldest son of Barnes Wallis of Dambusters fame), who first identified that BR were wrong in their analysis. (See Chapter Notes and inside of back cover).

British Rail and Ron Cotton

In late 1983, British Rail announced the appointment of Ron Cotton, an experienced railway manager, as Project Manager with a brief to close the line.

Again, if you need to know more about what happened, read Abbott and Whitehouse. The appointment later turned out to be highly significant. All lovers of the line will have a very soft spot for Mr Cotton.

Using every trick in the book

In a very short time Ron Cotton used every trick in the book that he knew to generate income for the line. By the time he retired in early 1987, revenue had quadrupled, services more than doubled - probably even better than when first opened - and eight stations had re-opened.

The discussions that BR had with TUCCs during this period were protracted. Ron Cotton may well have played a role in ensuring that more time was bought to generate additional income.

Impact on closure decision

It would have been difficult in 1989 for BR managers to argue that the line should close on grounds of cost when their principal argument had been lost.

Whilst within Whitehall or Westminster it was possible to get away with making an argument that the increased revenue came from people making their farewell railway journey, such an argument would not hold up under cross-examination at a judicial review.

Government and privatisation

One element that came into consideration in the 1980s was the potential privatisation of the line. Many resources were put into this approach.

In itself it was never realistic but, less than a month before the reprieve, local councils were arguing for a three way partnership involving the private sector as a way of avoiding closure.

Minded to consent to closure

In April 1988 the Secretary of State told Parliament that he was "minded to consent to closure". It brought a very sharp riposte from the Friends of the Line.

Freedom of Information Act

A short note about experiences of using the Act

The National Archives at Kew

The staff at the National Archives at Kew have been wonderful. Not only did they promptly send me a schedule of 50 open files, and 18 closed files, but they have assiduously helped me to get the Department of Transport to agree to open all these files, albeit it with some redactions. *Star rating 10/10*

The Cabinet Office

The Cabinet Office had been described by Rt Hon David Willetts, MP, and Minister for Science and Universities 2010-2014 as the most dysfunctional in Whitehall. The Institute for Government drew on the experiences of former Government Ministers and a summary was published in The Independent on 8th December 2015.

It matches my experience. A letter to the Department was ignored, a polite follow up to Rt Hon Francis Maude was ignored as was a letter to Matthew Hancock. MP after the 2015 election. Eventually contact via the Freedom of Information team brought some progress but no revelations at all. *Star Rating 3/10*

The Information Commissioner

There have been two referrals to the information Commissioner. Neither was satisfactory. My application to the Information Commissioner to release the Paul Channon letter was denied on the grounds that it was a small matter of no interest to more than a handful of railway enthusiasts, and the view that Cabinet Confidentiality would be broken if it were ever released and the whole basis of government would collapse. The letter was nevertheless released by the Department.

When I was getting nowhere with the Cabinet Office I politely asked if the Information Commissioner could actually do anything to get them to respond. A query was turned into a complaint which was then denied because I had not complained within 30 days notwithstanding the allowance I had made for "Purdah" when the government shuts down before an election. *Star Rating 4/10*

The Paul Channon Letter and other documents

After eventually discovering that such a document existed my first appeal was to the Information Commissioner. This was denied. A right exists to appeal to a Tribunal - called a First Tier Tribunal chaired by a judge with two lay assessors. Hearings can be held, or more often the panel makes up its mind on reading the papers. On making the final appeal we found out that the ICO was not to be represented, nor the Department for Transport. They argued for a paper hearing only. Thankfully the Tribunal, whose staff and Registrar could not have acted better rejected this and a Tribunal was fixed for 11th January 2016 in Leeds. We put our formal submission in on 17th November. Two weeks later the Department of Transport capitulated and produced the key document.

On hearing this and recognising that there was reference to legal advice, Edward Album put in his own FoI request. Eventually three documents emerged, one on the issue of bus substitution and the others commenting on the draft rejection letter.

Department of Transport

A curate's egg. It is brilliant that they have released the Paul Channon letter and agreed that 18 files at the National Archives can be opened. In addition they have released 8 pages of legal advice.

The Civil Service took over 16 months to release some earlier papers including the formal Civil Service Submission to Ministers. We have been told that no copy exists of the draft closure notice to which the lawyer writing on 29th March 1989 was responding. *Star Rating 3/10 & 7/10*

Mr Julian Smith, MP for Skipton and Ripon

The local MP Mr Julian Smith had been very helpful. Mark Rand, former Chairman of the Friends asked him to find what files were actually held by the DfT. Details of 6 files were provided by Claire Perry MP, Parliamentary Under Secretary of State. Eleven months later he did a follow up for me as I had by then moved home from Birmingham to North Yorkshire. *Star Rating 10/10*

Attorney General's Office

Enquiries brought a negative response. However it came with a wonderful caveat to the effect that the response should not be taken as implying that the Attorney General had not given advice. Even if he had they would not tell me. *Star Rating 5/10*

Overall Impression: Courtesy Rating Very Good - Decision making - Mixed

CHAPTER 5 PART 2
The Fight Back
The Community Responds

Yorkshire Dales National Park - DalesRail and Dalesman

Individuals in the West Riding Ramblers Association persuaded British Rail in 1974 to run a Ramblers special to stations closed in 1970. 500 people took part.

Later that year a number of authorities agreed to work together and the germ of the DalesRail service was born. By June 1975 this had been taken over by the Yorkshire Dales National Park Authority and by the end of the year nearly 5,500 passengers had enjoyed the experience.

One requirement (at least initially) of opening such services was that a National Park Ranger had to turn up with a torch to illuminate platforms if in the autumn services ran in the dark. In 1986 the Dalesman service saw eight stations re-opened.

Railway Development Society (later called Railfuture) and Transport 2000

There were two national groups with strong links in the North West. One was the Railway Development Society (RDS), with which John Betjeman was closely associated; the other was Transport 2000 (T2000), an advocacy group founded in 1972 from trade union roots pressurising for better bus and rail services.

Richard Watts was the indefatigable Chairman of the North West Branch of RDS, whilst T2000 was led by Dr John Whitelegg, an academic, and Peter Horton.

Friends of the Settle-Carlisle Line Association

The Friends of the Settle-Carlisle Line Association (later the word Association was dropped), had been formed in July 1982 with the primary purpose of safeguarding and promoting the Line.

They held their first meeting in Skipton. Many years later Gerry Thorpe, a Conservative Party Political Agent, told an AGM of the Friends how his bosses had asked him to "keep an eye" on what these people were up to. He expressed interest and sat in on meetings - but soon became a true believer and Vice-President of the Friends.

By 1984 membership of the Friends was 1,000. In April 1989 it had grown to nearly 4,500, the largest by far of the rail user groups in the country.

Brian Sutcliffe, Chairman of the Friends from early 1984, recognised that they had no experience as a pressure group and initially needed some direction. Under his chairmanship the Friends became a highly effective campaigning organisation.

Members came from many areas, and groups and the Friends developed links into Parliament, the Department of Transport and British Rail. From the outset they were quite clear that they would prefer to work with the grain rather than be a vociferous critic.

The Committee of the Friends during the main part of the campaign were all active, led by three individuals, Brian Sutcliffe as Chairman, Pete Shaw as Secretary and Edward Album as Legal Adviser.

Edward was a senior and experienced corporate lawyer in the City of London and, apart from legal issues, became the London end of the campaign with regular liaison with the Department of Transport, the Ministers and other leading political figures.

The Friends developed a valuable rapport with the leading civil servants and later with Michael Portillo when he became Transport Minister.

Pete Shaw was exceptionally knowledgeable about rail services and rolling stock movements and handled liaison with the press.

Brian Sutcliffe was a well-respected leader and was later honoured with the award of an MBE This, it was believed, recognised also the policy of the Friends to co-operate with the officials, where possible, without detriment to the objectives of the campaign, a policy which has been followed by subsequent Chairmen to the present day, including Mark Rand, Richard Morris and the present Chairman, Douglas Hodgins.

Joint Action Committee

In the early years of the campaign there were significant differences of views about the methodology of the campaign and the approach to be adopted.

There was recognition of the need for a single voice and the Settle-Carlisle Joint Action Committee was formed in early 1984 with five members including the Railway Development Society, Transport 2000 and The Friends. The Friends were represented by their Chairman, Brian Sutcliffe, and Philippa Simpson.

Peter Horton deserves great credit here as he master-minded the formation of the group. Later, Des Wilson, well known as a Liberal Party activist and a Freedom of Information campaigner, suggested a wider base and, by December 1985, a total of 18 groups ranging from Chambers of Trade to the Youth Hostels Association had acquired rights to Board Membership. (See Appendix 3).

The Railway Development Society was represented by Richard Watts. The Transport 2000 representatives, Dr John Whitelegg and Peter Horton took on roles as Chairman and Secretary and were effective leaders. The Railway Development Society and Transport 2000 were both experienced at closure campaigns.

Local Authorities working together

The Local Authorities (with, initially, the exception of the North Yorkshire County Council), all worked together closely and quite quickly put up £34,000 to enable PEIDA to undertake an independent assessment of the lines structures. PEIDA was an Edinburgh based company focusing on Planning and Economic Development consultancy. Their report was published in July 1984.

It should be noted that 15 Councils put money forward, as did British Rail, who felt the independent assessment would support their case (See Appendix 3). Brian Sutcliffe (Friends) is clear that Councillor Bill Cameron from Cumbria CC played a very significant role in the campaign.

Later the three County Councils, Cumbria, Lancashire and North Yorkshire, together put up £500,000 via the Trust (see below) towards the cost of repairs to the Ribblehead Viaduct.

Business Liaison Group presents a petition

The final campaigning group was the Business Liaison Group led by Ruth Annison (See Chapter Notes). It represented local businesses along the line and helped achieve the successful outcome. Michael Portillo still recalls being "Annissoned". Ruth Annison was indefatigable, writing letter after letter to the Prime Minister and many others.

Sophisticated Lobbying including Alan Bennett as a Yorkshire TV Film narrator

We can now see that in just over a year a sophisticated pressure group had been established with links into many parts of government. This was in an age before the internet and e-mails, or mobile phones. Occasionally someone had a fax machine!

There are two good illustrations. In 1985 Yorkshire TV made a regional programme lasting 15 minutes. Alan Bennett was the narrator and the film shows interviews with Peter Horton, Ron Cotton, Chris Wallis and Councillor Cameron. The quality of the programme stands out 30 years later.

Michael Portillo sees for himself - in the glare of local publicity

Three years later in 1988 Michael Portillo, who had become Number 2 at the Department of Transport, wanted to ride the line.

The Yorkshire Post records how, after taking a sleeper from Euston to Carlisle, he planned to take a train to Settle to see for himself. Someone either in BR or the Department leaked the information to the Joint Action Committee. (See Chapter Notes).

The Minister was greeted by camera crews and hundreds of people at every station waving banners with his name on them. Quite a feat of organisation and illustrative of the strength of support for the campaign.

Transport Consultative Committees (TUCCs)

We have seen earlier the role that had to be played by the Transport Consultative Committees. The early activities of the Friends and Joint Action Committee were aimed at getting as many people as possible to write to the TUCCs and participate at their hearings. The Friends were legally represented, as were British Rail.

Any closure proposal had to go before a TUCC. Under closure rules objectors could, in practice, question BR on all points regarding closure. This was not limited to any information provided in "Heads of Information". Crucially, however, BR did not have to respond, so in effect cross examination of BR figures was prohibited. The TUCCs believed that they could include reference to what they wanted in any report and that they were not limited to report on hardship issues. (See Chapter Notes)

Two TUCCs were involved. One was the Yorkshire Region (later the North Eastern) chaired by James Towler. His outspoken comments in favour of objectors did not go down well in London but were very well received by objectors and he injected clarity into the issues involved. Mr Towler did not receive a second term of office, but his work had been done. (See Chapter Notes).

For the North West TUCC Olive Clarke was the Chair. She conducted impartial and professional hearings and was well respected. The two TUCC chairpersons were completely in agreement in their conclusions.

BR issued three closure notices (see Chapter notes) not one of which complied fully with the requirements of the Act. In the end there were 32,000 objections to the closure proposals. The Secretary of State also received over 6,500 objections from individuals and a petition with over 40,000 signatures, including a paw print from the dog Ruswarp, to the Prime Minister.

First Legal Argument - Special Inquiry

The first legal argument put forward was that the Secretary of State should use his powers under the Transport Act 1962, Section 90 to order an inquiry into BR proposals.

Given that Nicholas Ridley - Secretary of State from June 1983 to May 1986 - had an antipathy towards the Settle-Carlisle Line it is not surprising this went nowhere. It was recalled that Mr Ridley had once said that the regular users of the line could be accommodated in a decent-sized minibus.

Legal Argument against Closure - BR Financial Case

BR had argued that the reason for closure was financial yet presented no figures to back this up. Initially the emphasis from the Friends at the TUCC hearings was on extracting from British Rail the actual figures for income and expenditure, including the real cost of repairing the Ribblehead Viaduct. It took two years for BR to provide the information.

Those leading the campaign used whatever resources and contacts they could to challenge BR. Indeed, the Friends had an opportunity in 1987 for a face to face meeting with BR.

Eventually, it was established that the Settle-Carlisle Line was one of the best performing rural lines in the whole network. Losses were small and could be reduced if account was taken of all potential revenue, including diversions, charter trains, and freight.

In fact, the Friends prepared a detailed analysis of present and future income and expenditure - supported by a leading commercial accountant - which was presented to the Department of Transport and given serious consideration.

Major features were contributory revenue from visitors from outside the area, from diversions and from goods traffic, which later was very substantial.

English Heritage: a possible crucial involvement through its largest grant ever

The involvement of English Heritage may have turned out to be crucial. In May 1987 English Heritage offered **up to £1 million** - its largest ever grant - towards the repair of Ribblehead Viaduct. Also significant was a grant of £100,000 from the Rural Development Commission.

Against the odds, the County Councils were prepared to contribute £500,000. One year later English Heritage produced a report which illustrated that BR's estimates for the cost of repair to the Ribblehead Viaduct were vastly overstated, whilst passenger journeys had increased to 450,000 and the revenue to £1,700,000.

Anniversary celebrations

The attitude of successors to BR changed. Twenty years after the reprieve of the line, celebrations were held on 25th April 2009. The Craven Herald reported that Jo Kaye, the Network Rail Route Director said:

"Had the line not been saved rail travellers would have been denied one of the world's most scenic railway journeys. Coal traffic from Scotland to power stations in Yorkshire and the Midlands would have had to use either the East Coast or West Coast Main Line, - both of which are heavily congested - and we couldn't have used it as a diversionary route."

There were further celebrations after 25 years, with the participation of the major personnel involved. A special train from Leeds-Carlisle had been organised. It carried 600 people with two Class 37's and a special headboard on the front. Ron Cotton and Michael Portillo gave speeches, and Olive Clarke (TUCC) cut the cake.

Settle-Carlisle Partnership and Association

When making the final announcement, Michael Portillo MP said he hoped that the vast public pressure that had helped save the line could be now used in a positive way to improve the line's future.

What happened has been a remarkable success story of collaboration between public and private bodies which has turned the Settle-Carlisle Line into a healthy and vibrant railway.

A loose association of the campaigning bodies acted in promoting discussion and possible solutions for the future of the line.

More recently, an umbrella organisation, the Settle-Carlisle Line Association, has been created under the Chairmanship of Bryan Gray, CBE.

The Association comprises:

- The Friends of the Settle-Carlisle Line
- The Settle and Carlisle Railway Trust
- The Settle-Carlisle Railway Development Company
- Settle & Carlisle Railway Properties Limited

The Settle-Carlisle Railway Development Company

For the record, the Settle-Carlisle Railway Development Company was formed in 1992 as a company limited by guarantee to encourage sustainable commercial developments on the Line.

The Settle and Carlisle Railway Trust

The Settle and Carlisle Railway Trust is a registered charitable Trust formed in March 1990. It was originally proposed in 1988 by Edward Album, Legal Adviser, on behalf of the Friends. This was put forward in a detailed communication to the Department of Transport at the height of the campaign to save the line and had the objective of bringing together various sources of funding, including the County Councils of Cumbria, Lancashire and North Yorkshire, and the West Yorkshire Passenger Transport Authority.

It was designed to offer the Government a material financial contribution to the repairs for Ribblehead viaduct. The contributions from the Trust for the Ribblehead Viaduct repairs eventually came to about £625,000 which, with the contribution of about £1 million from English Heritage, provided the major part of the eventual repair cost of £2.5 million. The proposal for the Trust was referred to in the Minister's announcement of the saving of the line and in the official letter to British Rail.

In general, the remit of the Trust was and remains to help preserve, restore and maintain historic buildings and structures along the line and to promote public knowledge and appreciation of the line.

The Department of Transport and County Councils assisted in the creation of the Trust. Initially with an independent Chairman, Denis Vernon, it had representatives from BR, the Friends and local interests. Later, the Friends' Legal Adviser, Edward Album, served as Chairman. The current Chairman is the former Bishop of Carlisle, the Rt. Rev. Graham Dow.

The Friends of the Settle-Carlisle Line

The Friends of the Settle-Carlisle Line was formed in 1982 to campaign against closure. Since1990 it has acted as a user group to improve facilities. It continues to be the largest such group in the country, with over 3,000 members. It was the main campaigning organisation and, with the Action Committee, bore the brunt of the campaign. The Friends have about 160 volunteers doing regular work and also play a vital part in reviewing services and franchises. A summary of the projects and activities completed by the various parties supporting the line is shown in Appendix 4.

If ever a railway support group deserved national recognition it is this partnership. *However, it is the links that they have built with other statutory bodies which mark it out as special.*

Over £100 million of investment by the Rail Authorities

In addition, there has been significant investment in freight, whilst British Rail, Railtrack and Network Rail have invested **over £100 million** in the infrastructure, especially track, signalling, safety and capacity. Illustrative examples are cited in Appendix 5.

CHAPTER 5 PART 3
Explanation
Run Up to the Reprieve Decision

Paul Channon letter to the Prime Minister - 6th April 1989

We now have the letter that Paul Channon wrote to Mrs Thatcher (for the Cabinet) on 6th April 1989 outlining his reasons for his proposed refusal to consent to closure of the line by BR.

However, before we get to that we need to look at the characteristics of earlier decisions by BR, the Government and campaigners from 1980 onwards. We will then explore what had changed between May 1988, when the Government was minded to close the line, and April 1989.

Earlier Decisions

What on earth led to the BR appointment of Ron Cotton as Project Manager to close the line?

BR announced the appointment of Ron Cotton as Project Manager in late 1983. By then, BR should have been aware that it was unlikely that the Settle-Carlisle Line would close quietly. They also knew what Ron Cotton's strengths were and understood that he did not necessarily reflect mainstream thinking.

So why was he appointed?

It appears that it was a consequence of organisational change that led to Mr Cotton's appointment. Mr Cotton had been selected to take on the post of closing the Settle-Carlisle Line and was told that this would take three to six months.

Ron Cotton had been a career railway man working in all five BR Regions. His bases had been Stratford, Kings Cross, Birmingham, Waterloo, Edinburgh, Newcastle, Liverpool and Manchester.

Ron recalls visiting a BR Board Member in London and suggesting that BR would be seen in a better light if at least some traffic was generated for the line. The Board member agreed. For three and a half years no one told Ron Cotton how to do his job. He was left to get on with it and in terms of generating traffic used every trick in the book.

With no objections from within BR he:

● **Introduced special cheap fares**
● **Introduced Round Robin tickets for longer distance travellers**
● **Ran extra trains**
● **Re-opened eight stations**

However, it is also very clear that Mr Cotton was fully representing the Board view about closure of the line to the public. At the end of the TUCC hearings, the barrister employed by BR told Mr Cotton: "Ron, I've represented lots of cases like this before but never as a junior."

Why did Ron Cotton act as he did?

Almost certainly, Ron Cotton acted as he did purely because it was the way he believed he should. The essentials of what he did had all been successful in his earlier career and, if others believed (as he did) that the line could have a future, then at the very least his job as the Railway Manager was to give that a chance to succeed.

Tactics employed by British Rail and the Department of Transport and the Treasury to close the line

Department of Transport and Treasury

In the Department of Transport, civil servants and Ministers would both have understood the formal distinction between their own role, which was to either turn down or ratify a BR closure proposal, or not to make the case for it at least until their own decision had been made.

However, that statement needs qualification in respect of the time when Nicholas Ridley was Secretary of State for Transport. The fact that no similar major closure had ever been turned down would not have been a factor in the decision. So the senior civil servant, the Permanent Secretary, would probably object to any allegation that his Department sought to close a line.

For those of us old enough to remember "Yes Minister", it is only too easy to see how civil servants can, on occasion, manipulate their political masters.

So whilst there were rational decisions, there were also organisational process issues and political ones, particularly when one remembers that Treasury civil servants would have been reminding their colleagues at the Department for Transport of the quid pro quo over a suspected agreement to electrify the West Coast Main Line to Scotland on the condition that the Settle-Carlisle Line would eventually close.

British Rail's constraints

British Rail was legally constrained in a number of ways, although for large parts of the campaign it seemed to believe that the end justified the means.

Had the BR attempt to persuade Cumbria County Council not to oppose the line closure been successful, the campaign against closure would have been greatly weakened. Many involved at the time believed that the BR Chairman, Sir Peter Parker, acted in good faith when he gave assurances that there were no plans to close the line. Does this mean that he was kept in the dark? Pete Shaw, former Secretary of the Friends, is not so sure. It could have been a play on words as "have no plans" can be interpreted in two ways.

There were certain consultative processes that BR had to abide by, particularly with the TUCCs. In that sense, part of their decision making, or more accurately their behaviour, was determined by organisational process issues. However, the way in which BR managers manipulated both the performance and general information in order to point to one logical - and from their perspective - *rational* decision, can only be described as highly political.

There are three possible explanations for this behaviour, not necessarily mutually exclusive:

1. A firm view that closing the Settle-Carlisle Line was a rational decision, taking reduction of government subsidies into account.

2. An attempt to repay Treasury civil servants for the quid pro quo of electrification of the West Coast Main Line to Scotland, and concern about the consequences if they did not.

3. An attempt by BR to extract additional money from the government.

What input did Ministers have into the discussions about closure?

During the 1980s a number of initiatives were considered. They almost all had political backing and included privatisation, the creation of linear theme parks, commercial sponsorship and use as a Heritage line. The seriousness with which these proposals were treated is illustrated by the willingness of Cumbria County Council in March 1989 to consider a three way partnership with British Rail and a private company.

Lazard's - sale of line

In August 1988 the merchant bankers Lazard Brothers, on behalf of the BR Board, produced a lavish brochure as a prospectus for the sale of the line. One organisation which came forward was a newly formed company called Cumbrian Railways. This was to be a tri-partite partnership between British Rail (at least initially), the County Councils and private interests. After initial support from the Joint Action Committee, it became increasingly unrealistic and as time went on no buyers of substance emerged.

In December 1988, a memorandum from Edward Album of the Friends stated:

"The Settle/Carlisle Line is not a self-contained entity, as some BR routes might be. The service is effectively not Settle to Carlisle but Leeds to Carlisle, with connecting services at either end. The conclusion is that this line is not suitable for separate ownership. Such ownership would mean costly duplication of administrative services, extra costs, and a loss of several sources of revenue if the line passed to a private owner. It is therefore unlikely to be viable on a long-term basis. On the other hand, the line is a viable and successful part of the National Network and can be further exploited as part of such network."

No government decision regarding a sale could be made, as the Secretary of State had to decide first if the line should close.

Issues raised by campaigners

Potential Legal Action
A partnership developed between the Friends and Cumbria County Council to pursue legal arguments.

Counsel
Senior Counsel (David Keene QC later Sir David and a High Court Judge) and Junior Counsel (Charles Flint now a QC) were instructed jointly by Richard Claydon and Edward Album on behalf of Cumbria CC and the Friends. Detailed instructions were given to Counsel with an explanation of the history of the campaign and the closure documentation.

The lawyers took the view that, if a decision in favour of closure were to be taken by the Department of Transport, a Court Application could be made for a judicial review, with a reasonable prospect of success.

The application would be based, inter alia, on the fact that since the closure notices had been issued, all the circumstances - including the potential revenues, the financial costs and the proposed alternative services - had changed and the closure proposal was no longer valid. A formal letter was drafted by Junior Counsel, but was not sent due to the reprieve.

Legal arguments
In essence the points being made were:

- The revenue earned by the line had increased substantially
- Costs of repairing infrastructure had reduced
- Eight stations had been re-opened
- Five trains ran each day in each direction - not the two when the initial case was put forward
- BR's case for closure was financial but they had failed to provide such information until February 1987
- BR wrongly asserted that the role of TUCCs was limited to hardship only
- Hardship had not and was not considered on a national basis
- Procedural flaws by British Rail had occurred, affecting the validity of closure notices
- Procedural flaws had been committed by Ministers, including a wrong view of government obligations if consent was refused
- Users of the eight re-opened stations had not had an opportunity to object to closure
- Connecting rail services had changed
- Alternative bus services had reduced drastically

- New and more efficient trains could be used
- BR's financial figures were disputed
- The right of users of diverted trains to object on hardship grounds was denied
- The proposal contained in the Lazard's document to sell to a private bidder meant that there would be no statutory right to object if a private rail service eventually failed, as closure would have already been accepted. In this connection it is interesting to note that the Lazard's sale document did not require a bidder to run any rail service at all

Judicial review

Although the formal steps preceding the judicial review were not taken, the Government and their advisers would have been well aware of the potential challenge. Indeed, they had specifically been informed of it by Cumbria Council. The Paul Channon letter confirms this.

If a judicial review had proceeded, it would have been accompanied by a demand for documents from British Rail and the Department for Transport and these would have had to be produced. The sale or closure of the line would have been halted in the meantime, and probably for an extended period.

Ribblehead Viaduct
The Friends led the co-ordination of fund-raising. Thanks to contributions mainly from English Heritage (up to £1 million or 40% of eligible costs, whichever was less) and from three County Councils (£500,000), together with a Rural Development Commission donation of £100,000, the net cost was likely to be around £0.9 million.

BR financial case
In October 1988 BR submitted a document to the Department of Transport. It was called "Financial case for the closure of the Settle-Carlisle Railway Line (updated)". The BR proposal was to close the Settle-Carlisle route but to provide a service three times a day between Leeds and Carlisle via Giggleswick, Carnforth and Penrith. BR's figures were strongly disputed by the Joint Action Committee and the Friends.

The BR document made reference to the fact that they had been offered a reduced cost of materials to repair the viaduct. This came from British Aggregate Construction Industries and the Federation of Resin Formulators and Applicators, who now join a roll of honour.

Joint Action Committee response

The Joint Action Committee produced a response in December 1988. The word closure had been replaced by retention. Their argument was that by using the Carnforth route BR would lose between £302,000 to £602,000. On their figures, retaining the Settle-Carlisle Line would bring in a profit of between £262,000 and £442,000 per annum.

How had the picture changed - May 1988 - April 1989?

It is worth looking briefly at what might have changed between May 1988 when the Minister was "minded to close" and April 1989 when the line was reprieved. Looking back, it seems that there could be six reasons for the change of heart:

1. Demolition of the BR case for closure, with increased traffic and reduced expenditure.

2. Fundraising initiated by the Councils and the Friends, especially for Ribblehead Viaduct.

3. The probability, if a closure decision had been made, of a bid for a judicial review being mounted by Cumbria CC and the Friends.

4. An offer by the Friends to set up a Trust to raise funds for Ribblehead and towards the other structures on the line.

5. Initiatives to promote and develop the line.

6 The failure to obtain any realistic offer to buy the line from a creditable organisation.

The final document seems to support this analysis. Certainly, the major funding provided by English Heritage, the Local County Councils, the Rural Development Commission and the Friends - together with the proposed formation of a Trust and a commitment to promote the line - helped Paul Channon and Michael Portillo in subsequent meetings with the BR Board.

CHAPTER 5 PART 4
The Final Decision
Summary and Reflections

The final decision

Key documents obtained

We now have copies of the key documents relating to the decision to reprieve the line from closure. They include the prior report to the Cabinet by the Secretary of State, Paul Channon (recently released pursuant to a Disclosure of Information request). Key documents are:

- The Secretary of State's message to the Prime Minister of 6th April 1989

- The announcement to Parliament on 11th April 1989

- The letter from the Department of Transport to the British Railways Board of 11th April 1989

- A preliminary letter dated 29th March 1989 - with many names redacted - commenting on a draft letter consenting to closure with conditions

- Civil Service - Final submission to Mr Portillo, 24th February 1989

Reasons for the 1989 reprieve

A comprehensive summary of reasons for the 1989 reprieve is contained in the letter to the British Railways Board of 11th April and in the previous message from the Secretary of State to the Prime Minister of 6th April.

Considerable trouble was obviously taken to set out the reasons for the decision both by the Secretary of State and the Minister for Public Transport (Michael Portillo) and by the civil servants at the Department of Transport.

In addition, the rights we have exercised under the Freedom of Information Act have produced comments on the judicial review and concerns expressed about the result. These documents come very close to the reprieve decision.

The main points which have emerged are the following:

1. Financial considerations

These are the key issues, as is always likely to be the case for Ministerial decisions of this type.

The three strands that make up the financial conclusions are:

(a) The re-assessment of the cost of repairing the Ribblehead Viaduct.
At the early stage of the closure process, this was put at between £5 million and £10 million. It is understood that the final figure was less than £2.5 million.

(b) Major contributions promised towards the repair cost for the Ribblehead Viaduct.
These contributions were up to £1 million from English Heritage, a total of £500,000 from the three County Councils involved and £100,000 from the Rural Development Commission.

(c) The improved revenue being received from the line, described by Mr Channon as up 50% from 300,000 journeys to 450,000 journeys per annum.
In fact, the Friends believe that the starting point before the full effect of the station re-openings and other improvements made by Ron Cotton was from about 150,000 journeys per annum.

The Secretary of State described the result as regards future earnings for British Rail as potentially a small loss or possibly even a profit with better marketing. In the case of the repairs for the Ribblehead Viaduct, over £1.6 million had been raised towards the final cost of approximately £2.5 million.

Credit for the improved financial position is partly down to Ron Cotton but also to the Friends and other campaigning organisations, which must have greatly helped to improve the usage of the line. The campaigning organisations also played a significant role in encouraging the contributions from English Heritage and the County Councils.

2. Absence of a bid for the line by private organisations

A determined effort had been made to sell the line to a private bidder but no creditworthy bids finally emerged. The position of a private bidder was always questionable in view of the cost of running the line as a separate unit that would need its own rolling stock, locomotives and staff and was therefore next to unsustainable. In fact, although an attractive prospectus was produced, a private bidder was not actually obliged to run any trains at all over the line, let alone any particular level of service. The absence of a private bidder was emphasised by the Secretary of State.

3. Legal challenge

As mentioned in the preceding parts of this chapter, preparations had been under way for some time for a legal challenge in the form of an application to the High Court for a judicial review if a decision to close the line were to be taken.

The legal work was done jointly by the lawyers for Cumbria County Council and the Friends. Junior Counsel and then Senior Counsel had been instructed. As mentioned by the Secretary of State in his message to the Prime Minister, the Department of Transport had been warned of this legal challenge and were not confident of a successful outcome. Such a challenge would have been a potential disaster, as it would have delayed the closure for many months, possibly for one or two years, and the decision of the Court may well have been to set aside the closure decision.

The impact of a judicial review is mentioned in the Secretary of State's message to the Prime Minister but not in the letter to British Railways or the public announcement. Nevertheless, it is believed to have been a highly significant factor in the decision.

4. Proposed formation of a trust fund

The Friends had proposed that a charitable trust be set up to raise funds on a continuing basis for the preservation of the historic structures on the line including, of course, the Ribblehead Viaduct.

This proposal was treated as a positive development by the Secretary of State and is specifically referred to in all three of the key documents. He said that he would support the proposal which, indeed, was fully implemented after the reprieve.

5. Bus substitution and legal opinions

Significant parts of the Paul Channon annexes address the issue of bus substitution. They show that Mr Channon is keen to make clear that his decision will not affect government plans to move some train services to buses. Here, he is reiterating government policy but at the same time making it difficult for Nicholas Ridley, a former Transport Secretary, to argue against his decision. Three letters from the Department's legal advisers - in December 1988 and March 1989 - spell out in detail what was being considered:

- Exploring the role of West Yorkshire Passenger Transport Executive in providing transport and possibly extending its boundary

- Finding out if a bus service could be reinstated after closure
- Comments on poor drafting, including paragraphs that contradict each other
- Facing up to the issue of hardship. If residents are suffering hardship, a bus service is necessary. If not, no service is needed
- Exploring narrow and wider definitions of hardship
- Querying the statement that "there is a strong possibility that the line can be run in the private sector"
- The need for proper, precise language when recommending closure
- Asking if one bus in the afternoon from Carlisle could really meet the needs of schoolchildren and commuters

6. Local support, particularly in the North of England

Other considerations referred to by the Secretary of State were the large number of objections, the opposition to the closure proposal from the Transport Users Consultative Committees and, more generally, the desire to avoid upsetting politicians and electors in the North of England.

The importance of these issues is difficult to assess but must have been a major factor with regard to the powerful and continuous campaign that had been waged by the local authorities and the many organisations concerned.

7. Other factors - not featuring in the official record

It is also interesting to look at those factors which did not feature - or did not feature prominently - in the announced decision. These include:

(a) Heritage and the natural attractions of the line

These factors were considered to be very important by the objectors but were not mentioned at all in the announcement of the reprieve or in the key documents referred to above. Whilst they must have provided an important background to the overall decision, they played no obvious part in the published decision, as compared with financial and legal issues.

Michael Portillo is on record (in the Yorkshire Post) as saying that heritage was a key factor. This might appear to be inconsistent with the published letter. However, this may not be the full story.

The decision that Paul Channon had to make was based on transport, not heritage, legislation.

Here, finance and hardship were the key factors. Had the Secretary of State used heritage as an argument against closing the line, he might well have been open to legal challenge from BR.

As the Secretary of State indicated, it was a matter of judgement. It is quite reasonable to believe that heritage contributed to the final decision.

(b) Value of the line for diversions and freight

The line had obvious value for diversions and for freight traffic, including the transport of imported coal, and subsequently these become important elements in the use of the line. We now know (see Chapter Notes) that the Government changed its mind about the way imported coal was to be transported from Hunterston to Drax and other Yorkshire coal power plants, and used the Settle-Carlisle Line for this traffic.

No evidence has been found to suggest that coal movement was a factor in the decision making, yet it may explain the alacrity with which BR and the Government spent money on the infrastructure.

(c) Politics

There are two possible angles here, one was a possible intervention by Lord Whitelaw; the other the need for the Conservative government to present good news.

Civil Service formal advice and issues arising

On 24th February 1989, J.R. Coates of the Railway Division produced a formal submission to Mr Portillo and Mr Channon (19 pages long with 12 annexes). The first page is shown in Appendix 9.

From it we learn that *in the Department's view the balance of probability is that on the basis of BR's financial case, as modified by the Department, the case for closure still stands (para 40) but either closure or retention could be justified on the facts.* The decision is therefore a matter of judgement of the likelihood one way or another (para 2).

The report is a good example of Civil Service practice. It was the culmination of five years of representations, statutory processes and analysis and was necessarily bulky. It was essential for both accountability and legal reasons that Ministers were able to say that they had considered all material relevant to the decision (para 1). We also learn that:

- The Secretary of State was not allowed to judge the case solely on policy grounds, as to do so would fetter the discretion conferred by statute, but he must have regard for railway policy (para 6)

- In October 1986 the Chairman of BR was told that the Government would continue to pay grant for "socially necessary services" and was not asking for a programme of major route closures (para 4). BR was required to reduce significantly its requirement for grant, and to review cases where attractive bus alternatives could meet the needs of travellers (para 4)

- In addition, the Transport Select Committee had been told that the justification for rail subsidy was seen as benefits for non-users - primarily for the relief of road congestion. Subsidy could also be justified for economically dependent communities. Normally, access needs should be met by bus services

Financial arguments: para 13 and Annex II

Financial issues were addressed under the following headings: On-line revenue; Contributory revenue; Ribblehead Viaduct; Other structures and maintenance costs; Substitute buses; Diversions.

Economic effects of closure: para 24-26

Reference is made to an English Tourist Board report. Employment Ministers had not yet taken a view, but economists had advised that the loss to the Exchequer was £3,000 per job and that, if the line were closed, the loss would be between £300,000 and £800,000 per annum.

Additional arguments

The most common additional arguments were in relation to the heritage value of the line's infrastructure (not, however, a proper use of Public Service Obligation grant) and the line's alleged profitable performance by comparison with other provincial lines (not relevant). Heritage aspects were recognised by English Heritage's offer of £1 million for the repair of Ribblehead (para 30).

Private bidders

The local authorities and other objectors are regarded as almost certain to seek a judicial review of a decision to close the line to BR services. The legal process might take a year. Lazard's advise us that a private bidder may not wait that long. Should a decision be made to give a private bidder powers to operate the line we would have to promote an order under the Transport Act 1981 which would be subject to negative resolution in either House. That also adds to the uncertainty (Annex XII para 8).

Business Liaison Group

The Business Liaison Group had an annex of its own. The group was organised by Ruth Annison (described as a trader in Hawes). The DfT assessment is that it is difficult to quantify the effect of closure on the local economy.

Earlier, civil servants at the DfT and the DTI had liaised over a submission made to the DTI, with the civil servant at the DTI accepting that Mrs Annison did have a point.

Friends of the Settle-Carlisle Association

Annex VIII is devoted to an analysis of points made to Mr Portillo on 8th December 1988. The final assessment from the DfT says: "Overall the work from FOSCLA adds little that is new to the evidence already submitted; it rearranges figures that originate elsewhere and presents them in an alternative form".

The relevant FOSCLA points were also considered systematically in Annex II - Financial Case. This particular assessment from the DfT is actually well wide of the mark. The first assessment of BR's true figures was done by Edward Album, Legal Advisor to the Friends and a Senior Chartered Accountant. These figures were used by other organisations until under the process of Sectorisation BR actually discovered the true costs.

Michael Portillo

It fell to Michael Portillo as Minister of State to make a recommendation to Mr Channon. We do not know what he said as no paper record has been found. It is of course conceivable that all of his communications with Mr Channon were personal and not via the Civil Service. Michael Portillo does not claim sole credit for the decision, but says **"the result bore my fingerprints"**.

Prime Minister

Paul Channon wrote to Mrs Thatcher on 6th April with his recommendation. A note from his Private Secretary on 10th April says that the Prime Minister agreed with his decision. Mr Channon had also written to the Prime Minister at the end of January 1989, indicating that the case for closure was less robust than before, with the major area of uncertainty being the likely revenue.

John Major

The Chief Secretary to the Treasury, John Major, requested that in his statement to Parliament that the Secretary of State did not "refer to benefits to the local economy as a reason for refusing consent because it might set an awkward precedent".

Sir Robert Reid - Chairman of BR

Paul Channon met Sir Robert Reid on 10th April 1989 to inform him of his decision. A detailed briefing note covers what was said. Mr Channon made the point that the current return fare of £7.60 should be raised.

The role of Lord Whitelaw

The Friends' archives have divulged several letters seeking his support, and one requesting his intervention directly with Mrs Thatcher (See Appendix 8). These approaches led to a meeting between Lord Whitelaw and representatives of the Friends.

Lord Whitelaw was given details of the Friend's arguments. He did make representations to the Prime Minister and personally received a letter from Paul Channon, Secretary of State on 11th April 1989. Yet again the DfT cannot locate the correspondence. He may well have been influenced by his direct personal knowledge of the area as a former MP for Penrith and the Border. It may be relevant that after the reprieve was announced, Lord Whitelaw became a Vice President of the new Trust.

Two sentences that help tell the story

The letter from Mr Channon to Mrs Thatcher contains two sentences: **"I am also doubtful about the wisdom of antagonising many in the North of England for such small and uncertain savings. I believe this doubt is shared by most of our colleagues in the House."** It is difficult to understand these sentences without thinking that the Whips Office were involved. Neither Lord Waddington, former Chief Whip nor Lord Garel-Jones, Deputy Chief Whip in the Commons, have any recollection of those events.

A difficult year for the Transport Secretary and the need for good news

We have already seen how the Transport Secretary, Paul Channon, had a difficult year. The Lockerbie Air disaster happened on 21st December 1988. The political fall-out from Lockerbie rumbled on and on, which was bad - or very bad - for the Conservative government.

Mark Rand, former Chairman of the Friends, wonders what the political consequences would have been of closing one of the three major railway routes from England to Scotland at such a time.

The need for good news is understandable. Not just that, as the Settle-Carlisle had by then acquired a place in the nation's heart. The Conservative government needed some good news and here it was on a plate.

The Settle-Carlisle decision was announced on 11th April 1989. In reality, three months after Lockerbie the position in the corridors of power had evolved from a preference to respect the quid pro quo over electrification by closing the line into a credible case for reprieve.

The decision in perspective

What railways are for

Finally, in looking at the decision, it is interesting to note that the Secretary of State continued to refer to a belief that the passenger operations of the railways exist basically for journeys for local people for employment or business. Apparently, tourism was not seen as a function for the nationalised railway but, rather, as something best taken care of by private companies. Most people would argue against this, on the basis that the railways exist to meet all types of needs including tourism.

Local authorities pushed to contribute

Another interesting factor is the serious attempt made by the Department of Transport to persuade the local authorities, particularly Cumbria County Council, to contribute on a continuing basis towards the annual cost of running the Settle-Carlisle Line. The local authorities were pushed very hard but were not prepared to give any open-ended undertaking to make revenue grants, as opposed to a fixed contribution to the Ribblehead Viaduct repairs.

Issues raised by release of legal opinions

The release of the legal opinions raise three issues:

Low level bus substitution

The civil servant making the request for a legal opinion asked "whether the Department could start with a low level of bus substitution service", adding "Can we get away without imposing a Settle-Giggleswick shuttle bus on the understanding that we can impose one later if necessary?"

Missing papers

Readers will have noticed from my experiences of seeking key documents through the Freedom of Information Act that a number of those I would have expected to find do not appear to exist. Whilst I might accept, for example, that Michael Portillo and Paul Channon kept their main recommendations away from the Civil Service, the number of missing papers does raise some eyebrows.

Late change of heart

It is clear that at least one team of civil servants were working on an expected closure decision on 29th March, just a few days before Mr Channon's letter to the Prime Minister.

That should not surprise or concern us. The last recorded decision of the Minister was in May 1988, when he indicated that he was minded to close. The fact that he had not yet considered all the extra information he had requested would be standard practice. However, it confirms the suspicions held for many years that, the Department was seeking to close the line. Indeed that was, on balance, their recommendation to Ministers. For some it came as a surprise. It is not possible from the official papers to say with certainty whether there was external intervention from either Lord Whitelaw or others. Michael Portillo is clear that the decision was taken in government prior to the letter of 6th April.

Summary

When was the real decision made?

Many earlier writings have suggested that it was unlikely the final key decision was made in the Department of Transport. The Paul Channon letter was written on the Thursday prior to the decision being announced in Parliament on the following Tuesday.

However it is clear that it was a decision taken in government, a decision that Paul Channon and Michael Portillo wanted, and that in seeking the Prime Ministers approval they were expecting a favourable response.

Reaction from BR and Government

There was a rapid response to the decision from BR and the government. BR moved quickly to implement the government decision. There are two possible reasons for this.

The first is that the BR Chairman Sir Bob Reid just told his staff to get a move on and - with a sense of history - "do an Allport".

The second explanation is that there was political pressure applied either on the coal or political front. Just as in the Beeching days when civil servants and Ministers saw eye to eye, so they did again. With no political dimensions to be concerned about, they simply got a move on.

Final evaluation

When the reprieve was announced, campaigners asked their Civil Service contacts "Why the change of mind?" The response was "Multiple Factors". I totally agree,

There are difficulties when advocates put forward 'single' explanation theories. For the Joint Action Committee, it might be the influence of all the protesters. For others, it might be the BR legal case blown out of the water. For Michael Portillo, it might be heritage.

All the theories need to be viewed together. The argument that the Government had run out of legal ways to close the line is almost certainly correct. This must have been a serious factor in consideration, given the potential judicial review. The financial evaluation was also crucial, and was heavily emphasised in Paul Channon's letter.

Leaving aside raw politics or even the issue of transporting coal, I think the government had no alternative but to reprieve the line.

In the end, a decision that may have been made with ill will was presented in a different light and all the organisations involved - BR, the Department of Transport and the Treasury - seem to have put their backs behind reprieve.

The model - three prisms

The model from Graham Allison offered three prisms through which to look at decision making. We shall consider them briefly.

Purely rational decisions

The Ministerial letter to Mrs Thatcher is full of decisions that fall into the category of 'rational actor' and 'rational response'. The financial case, the legal case, the inability to privatise the line and the use of Ministerial judgement - as well as the formation of the Trust - all point to purely rational decisions by government. To this we can add an element of government policy in supporting local communities.

Politics playing a part in decision making

The Paul Channon letter, with its explicit references to the North of England and the views of Conservative back benchers, shows political factors playing a part.

When the campaign started, the Settle-Carlisle railway was not lodged in the national collective memory as a gem. The strength of the whole campaign lay in changing official views. In this the Action Committee deserves credit. So too does Ruth Annison, of the Business Liaison Group, who personally sent individual letters  to 650 Members of Parliament. Her letter with her petition to the PM is enclosed as part of Appendix 8.

We saw earlier how individual participants in an organisation can play a political game. The way in which Sir Peter Parker was kept in the dark by his officials is a good example.

Decisions affected by organisational process

We have already seen how the issue of moving freight off the Settle-Carlisle Line to honour the understanding thought to be reached on the electrification of the West Coast Main Line meant that a fifteen year period elapsed before BR could credibly put together a closure case.

However, the sectorisation of BR by Sir Bob Reid meant that true information about the cost of Regional and Provincial Railways was available. As Edward Album indicates in his letter to Lord Whitelaw, the Settle-Carlisle Line was the best performing line in that portfolio, meeting 85% of its costs as against 35% for the Provincial sector as a whole and 82% for Network South East.

1980s campaign - reflections

A final reflection must go beyond the financial and legal considerations, important as they were. The tremendous strength of the campaign, coming from all levels of society and from all organisation affected, must also be taken into account.

The campaign was essentially just, reflecting not only on the outstanding beauty of the area and the engineering achievement but also the value of the line for practical purposes.

Impact of lobbying

This genesis of an idea for this case study started out with a thought about lobbying and whether there could be good or bad lobbying. We have seen the success of lobbying in 1869 - when the Midland Railway tried to get out of its obligation to build the line - and 1989. In 1869, the lobbying was by rail companies and landowners. In 1989, it was a broad-based public campaign.

However, it soon became clear that to understand what really happened over such a long time, we needed to go beyond this concept if we are really to our understand How? What? Why? and When?

Final words - from the Rt Hon Paul Channon MP

For once, shall we let the politician have the final word?
Paul Channon, in his statement to Parliament, ended by saying:

"I also look to the local authorities and others who have promised to support the line to work together to ensure that it has a successful future and so that the case for closure will not re-emerge".

APPENDIX 1
Decision Making Model
The model illustrated

Graham Allison in *Essence of Decision - Explaining the Cuban Missile Crisis* argues that a typically curious person - even an analyst - puts himself or herself in place of a nation or national government or indeed any type of organisation, asks "Why did so-and-so happen?" and then tries to figure out why a course of action was chosen.

This assumes that (in the case of governments, for example), the decisions came about as a result of purposive actions. The predominant model thus becomes the Rational Actor.

Allison suggests that this takes one so far - but not enough - and proposes three prisms:

- The Rational Actor - The classical model by which decisions are analysed
- Organisational Process Model
- Government or Bureaucracy Political Model

The Cuban Missile Crisis covered 13 days when the world stood still and waited. The saga of the Settle-Carlisle Railway has a history of over 130 years.

Graham Allison threw much new light onto the decision making processes in Washington, Moscow and beyond. In effect, he unpeels an onion - showing different layers. Here are four examples from his book.

Cuban Missile Crisis

Turkey - Jupiter Missiles
On becoming President, Kennedy ordered the removal of the Jupiter Missiles based in Turkey. In effect, they were beyond their sell-by date. He followed this up further. Down the line in the Pentagon and Defense Department, no action was taken as Turkey demurred. So it was that Kennedy found himself asking the USSR to remove the Cuban missiles, with the strong possibility the USSR would agree only if the USA removed the Jupiters. It would have been an awful climb-down. In the end such a claim was not made but the missiles were removed shortly after.

Blockade
He explores issues relating to the blockade. Armed forces generally require rules of engagement, with decisions not being referred up. One hell of an argument took place between McNamara and the Defense staff over this. By unpeeling the onion, Allison also discovers that David Ormsby-Gore, British Ambassador, had suggested that the intervention point be moved closer to Cuba to give more time for negotiations.

U2 Discovers Bomb Sites
Allison examines why they were found when they did. Because of the Gary Powers incident, the USA was cautious about flying too often over Cuba. Any photos also took between 9-12 days to analyse and to report to Washington. There were discussions as to whether or not the pilots should be in uniform. Either way it could well have been that the sites were not found until seven days later, which would have made discussions problematic.

USSR - Building of Sites
The USSR followed standard procedures in erecting such sites, with everything done in sequence. Had they changed their procedures, sites could have been ready before the USA discovered they were there.

We have seen how the model works.

- By showing clearly that organisations do not act as homogenous entities
- That different actors have different agendas
- That organisational process issues can affect the way decisions are taken

Settle and Carlisle Railway

We can look at examples relating to the Settle-Carlisle Line.

These examples also illustrate the strength of the theory. In so doing, it may be possible to rescue some reputations and to throw light not only onto the decision by the government to rescue the line in 1989, but the subsequent alacrity with which British Rail and others acted.

Specifically, we may look at the actions of **William Hutchinson** (Chairman from 1864-1870) and **William Price** (Chairman 1870-1873) in a new light, whilst the work by Kenneth Duffin in establishing a detailed early chronology of early events illustrates that commentators who suggested that James **Allport** "acted in a fit of pique" were well wide of the mark.

Here, we ask "Why Did William Hutchinson and William Price (Chairman) seek to avoid building the railway? Asking this question brings into play the relevant financial crisis of Overend and Gurney and the resignation of the whole Board of North British (a key ally) in 1866 for financial malpractice.

Each model asks different questions. For example:

Rational Actor

This model assumes that governments and others behave in wholly rational ways. One question might be "Explain why the Government abandoned plans to close the Settle-Carlisle Railway."

Perceived wisdom is that the government realised it had no room to manoeuvre and simply caved in.

However, as we shall see later, this explanation only takes us so far and at least two other hypotheses exist. The first relates to **raw politics and the fear of loss of Parliamentary seats**; **the second to the need to transport imported coal to power stations.**

This model alone is unable to satisfactorily explain why it was that British Rail, the Department of Transport and the Government moved so rapidly to rescue the line by investing millions of pounds in the infrastructure.

Organisational Process Model

This model challenges the assumption that every decision is taken by a unitary rational decision maker. In reality, organisations consist of autonomous groups and sometimes have semi-feudal elements. A classic example of the use of this model comes in understanding the work of the British Transport Commission after 1948.

So if someone was trying to understand why in 1953 the Churchill government decided to start breaking up the integrated system outlined in the 1948 Act, they might find that part of the explanation is what Kerry Hamilton and Stephen Potter in *Losing Track in association with Channel 4 1985* (quoted by Abbott and Whitehouse) describe as the "independence of outlook" operated by five transport executives in semi-feudal ways.

Another example comes shortly after the Beeching report in 1963, when Dr Beeching said the line should close. Following the 1968 accident between Horton and Ribblehead, Lt Col McNaughton, the investigating officer, said: "This route is planned for closure in the next few years". The first closure notice was published 15 years later. How do you explain this 15-20 year gap? It is unlikely that BR managers had a change of heart. The answer is to be found in the need that BR had to keep the line open for "unfitted" freight trains. Clearly a matter of organisational process.

If we go back much earlier to the 1860s, we note that after Parliamentary approval there were strict time limits for the purchase of land. Had Queen Victoria granted Royal Assent in 1866 as soon as the Bill came through Parliament, would there have been enough time in 1869 to complete land purchases?

Government or Bureaucracy Political Model

This model assumes no unitary actor. Rather, many actors as players with different agendas - in effect, political games involving trade-offs or wins and losses.

One good question is "Why was Sir Peter Parker, Chairman of British Rail, kept in the dark by senior managers over plans to close the Settle-Carlisle Line? Was he aware of the attempt to persuade Cumbria CC not to oppose the planned closure?

The disappearance of monopoly of transport meant that the common carrier policy from the 1850s had to go. Whilst some explanations are rational, there was clearly political gamesmanship going on.

If we try to understand the closure battle, we might ask "What was the role that Ron Cotton (appointed by BR in 1983 to close the line) played?" Abbott and Whitehouse describe his background and role in great detail. At the very least what emerges is an individual who thought and acted very differently from the prevailing BR culture. He has been described as a fifth-columnist.

Attractions of the model

Another of the strengths of the model is that it takes us beyond the more simple explanations sometimes given that focus on the question of lobbying. Certainly, the line would not have opened had it not been for strong lobbying in 1869, nor would it be open now without the successful campaign of the 1980s!

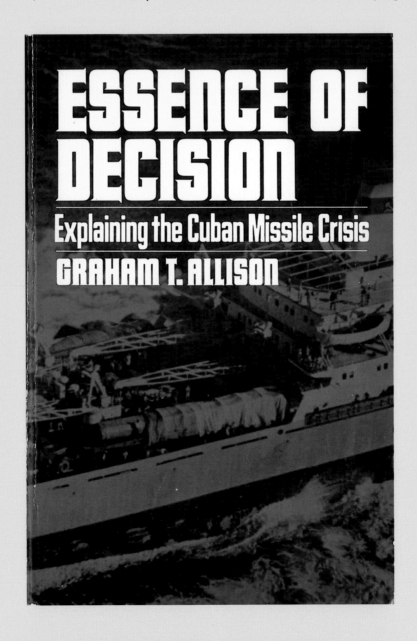

APPENDIX 2
Significant Dates 1962-1990
Thematic Presentation

Passenger Service Restrictions initiated by British Rail/Government

June 1966 - Clapham Junction to Low Gill closed as diversionary route.

Dec 1969 - Plans to close intermediate stations revived.

May 1970 - Local services were withdrawn from Horton, Ribblehead, Dent, Garsdale, Kirkby Stephen, Long Marton, Newbiggin, Culgaith, Langwathby, Little Salkeld, Lazonby & Kirkoswald and Armathwaite.

1974 - Downside platform at Ribblehead removed to improve access to BR ballast quarry.

1974 - BR claim that in order to provide a diversionary route for West Coast Main Line platform edges on disused stations needed to be removed to allow clearance for new Mk111 coaches. This was not implemented.

1974/5 - BR try and fail to impose higher safety standards on DalesRail.

May 1976 - New timetable means end of Thames-Clyde Express and other St Pancras-Glasgow trains.

May 1977 - Remaining service from St. Pancras to Glasgow withdrawn.

May 1981 - Plans to divert Nottingham-Carlisle Service become known.

May 1982 - Last Nottingham-Glasgow express trains run over Settle-Carlisle Line.

Apr 1989 - BR slaps 25% surcharge on weekend charter trains.

Passenger Service Developments

1964 - In November the Labour Government refused authority to proceed with withdrawal of local services.

1974 - Late Summer rambler's special calls at stations closed in 1970. 500 ramblers take part.

December 1974 - Meeting at Settle lays basis for DalesRail services. BR, Cumbria County Council, Eden District Council and United and Ribble bus companies work together,

May 1975 - Yorkshire Dales National Park Authority runs first DalesRail service to Dale's stations closed in 1970 plus Kirkby Stephen and Appleby. Two trains on Saturday and one on Sunday started from Leeds and Bradford. By the end of the year 5,497 passengers had been carried.

May 1976 - DalesRail extended to Carlisle and stops at Armathwaite, Lazonby & Kirkoswald and Langwathby.

May 1977 - West Yorkshire PTE takes on marketing of DalesRail service.

March 1978 - Steam returns to the Settle-Carlisle Line as BR approved route.

November 1983 - All West Coast Main Line services diverted onto Settle-Carlisle Line due to failure on overhead wires.

July 1984 - Huge demand prompts introduction of additional York-Carlisle daily return train.

December 1984 - BR says Settle-Carlisle Line Revenue up by 80% on 1982 figures.

Winter 1985 - Ron Cotton introduces £5 Saver.

December 1985 - BR says passenger numbers up 20% on 1984.

July 1986 - Dalesman service launched bringing re-opening of 8 stations previously used only by DalesRail.

February 1987 - Ron Cotton retires. Services have doubled and revenue quadrupled.

May 1987 - BR launches most comprehensive local timetable ever seen. It means that in 12 months time the line will carry 500,000 passengers in a year.

January 1988 - Landslip at Mallerstang. Quick repair suggests reprieve possible.

Goods and Quarry service changes

1964 - Goods services withdrawn from stations served only by local trains.

October 1970 - Settle Station closed to goods traffic.

September 1971 - Appleby Station closed to goods traffic. Dairy siding had been used since 1930.

1975 (approximately) - Long Meg anhydrite mine sidings closed.

May 1976 - around 13 freight trains a day in each direction transferred from West Coast Main Line as unfitted freight.

1982 - Quarry siding at Horton in Ribblesdale closed to help justify closure.

May 1983 - Last through freight services diverted from Settle-Carlisle Line.

March 1989 - BR announces closure of Warcop to Appleby Line carrying Ministry of Defence trains.

Closure Information and Notices

In 1968 an accident between Horton and Ribblehead injured two people. Lt Col I.K.A. McNaughton who investigated the accident reported on plans for eventual closure. Even if the Settle and Carlisle railway was planned to be part of the long term railway network it would still come low on the priority for installing AWS . **"This route is planned for closure in the next few years".**

Early in 1981 - Cumbrian MP's told of concerns re structures on the line.

April 1981 - Steam World article says that Ribblehead Viaduct needs to be replaced.

July 1981 - Chairman of BR - Sir Peter Parker makes first of many assurances that Settle-Carlisle Line will not close.

August 1981 - Confidential BR document links Ribblehead viaduct question into whether line is needed at all and predicts closure by 1984.

March 1982 - MP's told in confidence in Preston that closure of line is planned.

August 18th 1983 - BR says it intends to close the Settle-Carlisle Line.

November 17th 1983 - BR announces Ron Cotton had been appointed as Settle-Carlisle Project Manager with brief to close the line.

Dec 15th 1983 - BR publishes closure notice.

April 1984 - First closure notice withdrawn.

May 1984 - Sian Johnson and Associates announce plans for Settle-Carlisle Line to become linear theme park with privatised railway.

May 1984 - 2nd closure notice published. Transport Minister visits Ribblehead Viaduct.

August 1984 - 3rd closure notice published.

March 31st 1987 - James Towler "sacked" as Chairman of North-East TUCC.

April 1987 - Public Transport Minister finds standing room only on train from Settle.

May 14th 1987 - Ideas for commercial sponsorship.

July 1987 - Further information comes out on possible privatisation.

July 31st 1987 - Firm decision imminent. Betting now is on closure with time to investigate privatisation proposal.

November 1987 - News of possible rescue package based on job creation programme by the Jarvis group.

December 1987 - BR admits viaduct not falling down - but subsequently denies reports.

May 1988 - Anticipated reprieve becomes "minded to authorise closure".

May 1988 - Private bids invited.

June 1988 - TUCC's rule out new hearings.

July 1988 - Michael Portillo becomes new Transport Minister. Grants reprieve to May 1989.

August 1988 - BR offer sales prospectus for sale of line with very restrictive conditions.

August 1988 - TUCC's promise to go for new hearings.

September 1988 - An extra six months for private bidders allowed.

The Fight Back

June 27th 1982 - Inaugural meeting of the Friends of Settle-Carlisle Line Association.

March 1983 - Railway Development Society launches campaign to save line.

May 1983 - Joint Action Committee brings together Friends of Settle-Carlisle Line, Transport 2000 and Railway Development Society as campaigning umbrella.

December 1983 - Joint Council's campaign launched with running of Cumbrian Mountain express.

December 1983 - Joint Council's Commission PEIDA Report.

Feb 1984 - NUR launches campaign with special train.

July 1984 - PEIDA Report published. Illustrates wanton neglect by BR - Ribblehead viaduct can be repaired.

Aug 1984 - Joint Action Committee forms limited company.

Dec 1985 - Joint Action Committee AGM gives 18 groups rights to membership.

Dec 1985 - Plans to launch station re-opening campaign announced.

Jan 1986 - House of Commons Select Committee warns of danger to tourism if line closed.

Mar 1986 - West Yorkshire steam special runs as prelude to Council input into TUCC meetings.

March 1986 - West Yorkshire County Council et al expose closure by stealth policy.

March/April 1986 - North West TUCC hearings in Appleby and Settle.

Dec 1986 - TUCC report condemns BR closure case.

Jan 1987 - Friends of Settle-Carlisle Line launch major challenge to financial case for closure.

May 1987 - English Heritage offer £1m grant to repair cost of viaduct. Offer lies in Dept of Environment in tray for 6 months.

Aug 1987 - Councils offer continued revenue support.

April 1988 - Councils offer £500,000 to repair Ribblehead viaduct.

May 1988 - Threats of legal action from Councils and the Friends.

October 1988 - English Heritage report says repairs to viaduct will cost £2.5m - much less than BR estimates.

5th January 1989 - Edward Album, Legal Advisor to the Friends seeks help from Lord Whitelaw.

16th January 1989 - Ruth Annison on behalf of the Business Liaison Group lobbies Mrs Thatcher.

29th January 1989 - Secretary of State, Paul Channon writes to the Prime Minister, Margaret Thatcher to tell her that the BR case was not as robust as originally thought.

24th February 1989 - Final Civil Service submission to Ministers goes to Michael Portillo, Minister of State.

March 1989 - Councils suggest 3 way partnerships with private company to run the line.

28th March 1989 Legal Advisor sends 5 page letter on draft Settle-Carlisle Decision letter which recommended closure.

6th April 1989 Secretary of State, Paul Channon writes to the Prime Minister, Margaret Thatcher, outlining the reasons why he has decided not to consent to BR Closure proposal.

10th April 1989 Prime Minister consents to reprieve.

April 11th 1989 - Reprieve announced

APPENDIX 3
Settle-Carlisle Joint Action Committee
Membership December 1988

Appleby in Westmorland Chamber of Trade
Appleby in Westmorland Town Council
Council for the Protection of Rural England (Craven)
Friends of the Settle-Carlisle Line Association
Railway Development Society
Ramblers Association
Settle Chamber of Trade Settle Community Council
Settle Town Council
Skipton Town Council
Transport 2000 Derbyshire and Peak District
Transport 2000 North Lancashire and Cumbria
Yorkshire Dales Society
Yorkshire Rural Community Council
Youth Hostels Association (North Region)

Parish Councils
Crosby Garrett, Culgaith, Dent, Gargrave, Great Salkeld, Hawes and High Abbotside, Hellifield, Horton in Ribblesdale, Kirkby Malhamdale, Kirkby Stephen, Langcliffe, Lazonby, Long Marton, Sedbergh, Wetheral.

PEIDA REPORT INDEPENDENT STUDY 1983
Funding

County Councils
Cumbria, Lancashire, West Yorkshire

District Councils
Bradford, Calderdale, Carlisle, Craven, Eden, Leeds, Pendle, Richmondshire

Others
Settle Town Council, the Countryside Commission, English Tourist Board, Yorkshire Dales National Park Authority and British Rail

APPENDIX 4

Settle-Carlisle Line Partners and Associated Bodies including the Railway Heritage Trust (RHT) The Settle-Carlisle Railway Development Company, the Settle and Carlisle Railway Trust and the Friends of the Settle-Carlisle Line

Projects and Activities from 1990

Building-related

- Contributions to Ribblehead Viaduct Repairs
- Re-instate northbound platform at Ribblehead
- Acquisition by the Trust of 125 year leases of Ribblehead, Horton-in-Ribblesdale and Kirkby Stephen stations and restoration and conversion of station buildings with major contributions from the RHT and EU Development Fund
- Kirkby Stephen Footbridge funded by the Friends
- Ribblehead Visitors Centre created by the Trust and funded by the Trust, Friends and others
- Station Master's House, Ribblehead acquired freehold by the Trust. Funded by the Trust and Friends and a book room restored with a major contribution from the RHT
- Appleby Station - Major upgrade by **Network Rail**
- Settle Station - Major upgrade by **Network Rail** including footbridge and disabled toilets
- Garsdale Station - Waiting Rooms rebuild
- Hellifield (off the line) - Major refurbishments by **Network Rail**
- Waiting Shelters at Dent, Kirkby Stephen, Langwathby and Lazonby part funded by outside bodies
- Carlisle Station Gateway to the Settle-Carlisle and Newcastle Lines. Arch on platforms 5 and 6 assisted by the Friends
- Heritage Lighting
- Heritage Clocks
- Signal boxes at Armathwaite and Settle
- Station Gardens and flower beds
- Station Painting
- Weather station - Ribblehead

Other Activities by the Friends, Trust and Development Company

- Tourism Strategy - passenger numbers up from 450,000 to 900,000
- Design Guide for stations
- On train trolleys
- On train guides
- Guided walks programme - 20 experienced leaders
- Funding - Guided walks programme
- Full colour brochures and timetables twice a year
- Expanding ticket sales at Settle and Appleby (extra staff)
- Operate Dales Railcard
- Organise group bookings
- Magazines to over 3500-4500 people
- Teacher education packs
- Shops at Settle and Appleby Stations
- Visitor centres
- Historical Research including Archive at Horton-in-Ribblesdale Station
- 160 regular volunteers

APPENDIX 5
Settle-Carlisle Railway

Freight - Engineering and Infrastructure - Capacity and Safety Developments by Freight Companies - BR - Railtrack - Network Rail as well as franchise holders

Freight - Settle-Carlisle Line Originating
Fly ash trains to Kirkby Thore
Trains from Ribblehead siding taking timber to Chirk - North Wales
Timber from Kingmoor (Carlisle) depot to Chirk (North Wales)

Freight using Settle-Carlisle Line as Through Route
Coal from Scotland (mainly Hunterston) to Yorkshire power stations
Northbound movement of containerised domestic fuel (now ceased)
Engineering train weekday afternoons in preference to WCML with scrap ballast, sleepers, etc.
Cement from Horrocksford (Blackburn Line) to Scotland
All freight balanced by movement of empty wagons on return journey

Engineering and Infrastructure Developments since 1989
Relaying of 72 miles of track after 1996 coal train derailed near Dent Head
Ribblehead Viaduct refurbished and some others including Arten Gill
Kirkby Thore project to stabilise ground and remove long standing speed restriction. Problem resulted from gypsum mining subsidence
Ground stabilisation work on the sides of cuttings, especially at Blea Moor and north of Kirkby Stephen

Capacity and Safety Developments
Replacement of semaphore distant signals with colour sign signals and installation of AWS - automatic warning system
Installation of radio masts along the line giving reliable" ship to shore" communication between trains and controllers
Capacity improvement by installation of IBS (intermediate block signals) between a number of signal boxes to improve headway between following trains - cut from 25 minutes to 10 minutes
Portakabin signal box at Kirkby Thore for new gypsum siding, also cutting in half the old Appleby-Culgaith section
Turn back signal at Blea Moor to speed up turn round of train termination at Ribblehead
Passenger footbridges at Settle and Kirkby Stephen

Useful References - Freight Contacts
Freightliner Heavy Haul, DB Schenker (took over from EWS) GBRF (Great Britain Railfreight) and DRS (Direct Rail Services) and Colas Rail. In addition, the Rail Freight Association (RFA) is a trade and lobby group with a good reputation.

APPENDIX 6
Selected Bibliography

SELECTED BIBLIOGRAPHY

OFFICIAL RECORDS

Department for Transport

6th April 1989 - Two page letter and six page annex headed SETTLE-CARLISLE RAILWAY from Rt Hon Paul Channon, Secretary of State to the PRIME MINISTER.

24th February 1989 - Final Civil Service Submission to Mr Portillo, Minister of State.

28th March 1989 - Five page letter from LEGAL ADVISOR (name redacted) to (redacted) on SETTLE-CARLISLE: DECISION LETTER including reference to low level bus substitution.

15th December 1988 - Three page letter from LEGAL ADVISOR (name redacted) to (redacted) on SETTLE-CARLISLE RAILWAY on Passenger Transport Executive boundaries.

14th December 1988 - One page letter from LEGAL ADVISOR (name redacted) to (redacted) on SETTLE-CARLISLE RAILWAY On PTE boundaries.

ARCHIVES

The National Archives at Kew, Richmond, London have been an invaluable sources as the Department of Transport has opened 18 previously "closed" files.

Archives of the Friends of the Settle-Carlisle Line.

BOOKS

ABBOTT, Stan and WHITEHOUSE, Alan. *The Line that Refused to Die.* Leading Edge Press & Publishing, Hawes, North Yorkshire, 1990.

ALLISON, Graham T. *Essence of Decision - Explaining the Cuban Missile Crisis.* Little, Brown and Company, Boston, 1971.

ANDERSON, V.R & FOX, G.K., *Stations and Structures of the Settle & Carlisle Railway.* Oxford Publishing Group an imprint of Ian Allan Publishing, Surrey, 2nd Edition 2014.

BAIRSTOW, Martin. *The "Little" North Western Railway.* Martin Bairstow, Leeds, 2000.

BAUGHAN, Peter E. *Midland Railway North of Leeds - The Leeds-Settle-Carlisle Line and its Branches.* David and Charles Publishers, Newton Abbott, Devon, 2nd Edition 1987.

CONOLLY, W Philip. *British Railways Pre-Grouping Atlas and Gazetteer.* Ian Allan Publishing, Horsham, Surrey. 2011 reprint of 1958 edition.

DUFFIN Kenneth D. *The Man from Tasmania.* Privately Published, Budleigh Salterton, Devon, 2012.

ELLIS, Hamilton. *The Midland Railway.* Ian Allan, London 4th edition, 1961.

HENNESSY, Peter. *Never Again, Britain 1945-51.* Jonathan Cape 1992; Penguin Books, London, 2006.

HOUGHTON F.W and FOSTER W.H. *The Story of the Settle-Carlisle Line.* Norman Arch Publications, Bradford, 1948.

JENKINSON, David. *Rails in the Fells - A Railway Case Study.*
Peco Publications and Publicity Limited, Beer Seaton, Devon 2nd Edition, 1980.

PEARSON, Michael - *Pearson's Railway Rides - Leeds-Settle-Carlisle.*
JM Pearson and Son, Tatenhill, Staffordshire 2nd Edition, 1993.

SHARPE, Brian. *Settle & Carlisle Revisited - The Line that Refused to Die.*
Morton's Media Group, Horncastle, Lincolnshire, 2012.

TOWLER, James. *The Battle for the Settle & Carlisle.* Platform 5, Sheffield, 1990.

ARTICLES

CUMBRIAN RAILWAYS ASSOCIATION. *Obituary Peter Robinson* 8th August 2014.

ELIOT, Geoffrey. *Don't Panic we've seen this before.* Daily Telegraph, 19th September 2007.

GIBBINS, E.A. *CMIT Railway Nationalisation, Transport Myths and Mistakes.*

HERBERT, Ron. *The 1970s closure plan.* Rail Magazine No 746, April 16th - 29th 2014.

PICKFORD-JONES, Tim and Timmonet. *Dr Beeching - The Railway Axe Man.*
Newcastle upon Tyne, 2013

RAND, Mark. *Hopes for New Quarry Traffic.* Friends of the Settle-Carlisle Line,
Quarterly Magazine, November, 2013.

RATCLIFFE, Roger. *Holding the line. Looking back on the political battle to save the Settle-Carlisle.
Roger Ratcliffe talks to Michael Portillo.* Yorkshire Post Magazine March 29th, 2014.

ROBINSON, Peter. *The Settle & Carlisle Line.* Modern Railways May 2014.

SHAW, Pete. *The Day I joined up - Recollections.* Friends of the Settle-Carlisle Line,
Quarterly Magazine, August 2011.

SUTCLIFFE, Brian. *The Friends in the 80's - Recollections.* Friends of the Settle-Carlisle Line,
Quarterly Magazine, August 2011.

CHAPTER NOTES

Chapter 1 - Introducing the Decision Making Model

Graham Allison p 1
Graham Allison says that his book originated in early discussions between academics of the impact of bureaucracy on policy. More specifically, the gaps between what the principal actors wanted and the result of their actions.

Chapter 2 - Birth of a Railway

Chronology pp 3-10
In terms of chronology there is heavy reliance on Kenneth Duffin. The Man from Tasmania, Chapter 12 - A Pioneer Appears on the Scene and Chapter 13 - Years of Uncertainty - are particularity relevant.

Cost of railways p 4
Country comparison costs per mile in 1860 come from Dr Marjorie Bloy - A Web of English History - The Peel Web - a resource for students covering the Age of Peel 1830-1850.

James Allport entered into an agreement with Great Northern Railway in 1858 for Midland Railway to have direct access to London via Kings Cross for £20,000 p.a.

Updated costings come from Gregory Clark, What were the British Earnings and Prices then?

Parliament pp 6-8
Peter Baughan. The Midland Railway, is very helpful. Chapter 1X. The Settle and Carlisle Bill 1866 pp133-146 and Chapter X11 - Abandonment Foiled, are relevant.

Act of Parliament 1866 p 6
The full title ran as follows - An Act for enabling the *Midland* Railway Company to construct Railways from *Settle* to *Hawes, Appleby* and *Carlisle*: and for other Purposes. (16th July 1866).

Overend and Gurney p 7
It is worth reading Geoffrey Eliot, a retired City and Wall Street banker. Writing in the Daily Telegraph on 19th September 2007, under the heading "Don't panic we've seen this before", he draws on his more substantial work, *The Mystery of Overend and Gurney a Financial Scandal in Victorian London,* 2006.

Building the Railway p 9
See David Jenkinson in the section The Line and Its Environment. The geological background pp12-17. The railway in relation to the evolution of landform pp18-38 and the Railway Landscape - The line itself pp39-46.

Chapter 3 - Consolidation and Nationalisation

Local Traffic p 16
Go to David Jenkinson Part 111 Local Traffic Patterns pp95-116.

Common Carrier Policy p 17
The Railway and Canal Transport Act of 1854 (introduced by Viscount Cardwell, Board of Trade President) designated railways and canals as common carriers transporting goods and passengers for the common good. An obligation was placed on operators to offer fair services. It was repealed by the Transport Act of 1962.

Railway Nationalisation p 19
Significant information comes from EA Gibbins, CMILT, who has written on Transport Myths and Mistakes, including Railway Nationalisation. He took early retirement from BR. His last post was Chief Officer, Quality of Service. Year of writing not clear.

Winter of 1947 p 19
Houghton and Foster (p89) tell of how one day over 1,000 loaves of bread were baked in Skipton and taken up to Horton-in-Ribblesdale. Within minutes the Station Master found half the village beside him as he distributed on the basis of 4 for Metcalfe, 3 for Smart, 7 for Martin etc., as he knew each family.

Monopoly Disappears - Herbert Morrison p 20
Commercial use of Roads. The Times, February 15[th]1933.

Chapter 4 - The Run up to Dr Beeching

Beeching - Stedeford Report p 22
The report was so secret that when Barbara Castle became Minister of Transport in 1966 she was not allowed to read it. Source is David Henshaw in his 1994 book The Great Railway Conspiracy.

Dr Richard Beeching p 23
Was he sacked? Reports in The Times on 17th and 18th November 1965.

The Civil Service p 25
Peter Hennessy pp379-380.

Ruswarp p 26
Graham Nuttall, first Secretary of the Friends, and his collie dog Ruswarp (pronounced Russup) were inseparable. As a fare paying passenger Ruswarp was able to register his objection to the closure. Shortly after the line was reprieved, Graham and Ruswarp were walking in the Welsh Mountains. Graham never returned. After 11 winter weeks Ruswarp was found with his master. At the funeral as the curtains closed he gave a long, low muffled howl. Sadly, Ruswarp died soon after but a sculpture at Garsdale Station recalls his story.

It is had on good authority that, when BR managers read of his signing of the petition, they were told that Ruswarp's fares would not be credited to the Settle-Carlisle Line as he was on a Rover ticket!

Chapter 5 - National and Local Narrative

Dialogue of the Deaf - London Beer p 27
Simon Bradley - St Pancras Station - (Profile Books 2007) p70.

Miles of Track and Passenger Numbers p 27
Basic information can be found in the Annual Reports of the British Transport Commission and of British Rail.

Conservative Initiatives p 28
The quote comes from Christian Woolmar p50 in his book *On the Wrong Lines* Chap 3. Mr Ridley was told not to raise the matter again. By 1990 Mrs Thatcher had changed her mind. Two main achievements of the Conservative government were the electrification of the East Coast Main Line and the building of the Channel Tunnel.

Transport Users Consultative Committees p 30
The rules on cross examination applied equally to roads, as no one could cross question the Ministry of Transport on their estimates for new roads. Eventually, with the Winchester by-pass scheme, protesters realised that by rioting and stopping meetings from finishing, the process could go on forever.

Diversionary route for West Coast Main Line p 30
Nearly 25 years after Beeching nothing had changed, as J.R Prideaux, Director of Inter-City trains abruptly told C.G Lewin, (Co-Ordinator of Private Capital on 5th July 1988) to get lost when Mr Lewin had asked if the potential private bidder could expect income from a diversionary route. Source: The National Archives.

Freight - 20 year wait p 31
Lt Col I.K.A McNaughton was Chief Inspecting officer for Railways. The full title is *Report on the Collision that occurred on 30th October 1968 at Selside near Horton-in-Ribblesdale in the London Midland Region of British Railways*. HMSO. The quote comes from p40.

Unfitted Freight p 31
Information from Roger Goode.

Sir Robert Reid p 31
It is difficult to overstate the importance of the move to decentralisation. Gradually. BR HQ Management moved on and by 1987 the Provincial and Regional Sector found it had inherited a proposal to close its most cost-effective line.

Peter Robinson - BR Manoeuvres to close the line p 32

Peter Robinson played a significant role in the early management of the Settle and Carlisle Railway Trust. He worked for a number of years as Chairman of the Trust Executive, and was the right hand man of the Trust Board Chairman, ensuring that things got done.

Chris Wallis - Ribblehead Viaduct p 32-33

Chris Wallis had worked for BR for 13 years with a focus on bridges before setting up his own company to restore historic buildings. When with BR he had argued that the in-house argument for closing the Barmouth viaduct on the Cambrian Coast Line was false. Subsequently, it was repaired at a quarter of the original BR cost. On hearing of the issues with the Ribblehead Viaduct, he felt the same tactics were being used.

In an article in New Civil Engineer he described BR tactics as a red herring. All that was needed was to fill the hollow piers with concrete, add cross-bracing where needed, treat external cracks with resin grout, and lay a new waterproof decking on top. Best source is James Towler p 82, and pp 216-218.

Chapter 5 - Part 2 - The Fight Back - The Community Responds

p 35 onwards

Significant input from Edward Album, Archives of the Friends and Abbott and Whitehouse.

Friends of the Settle-Carlisle Line Association p 35

Information from Edward Album.

Joint Action Committee p 35-36

Dr John Whitelegg, founding Chairman of the Joint Action Committee, provides the introduction to Abbott and Whitehouse. In addition, many more references from Abbott and Whitehouse.

Glare of Publicity p 36

Pete Shaw, previously Secretary of the Friends (in conversation with the author at a windswept Garsdale Station), recalled what happened. The Joint Action Committee had access to an office and a phone at Lancaster University, where Dr John Whitelegg was based. One evening there were five people in the room when the phone rang.   Later someone listened to the message and suddenly five individuals were doing their utmost to organise the next day's activity.

Business Liaison Group p 36

Ruth Annison was the Chair and driving force behind the Business Liaison Group. In 1975 in her mid-30s, she and her husband, both college lecturers, acquired the Outhwaite rope-making factory in Hawes. Once the Settle-Carlisle Line was saved, Ruth Annison turned her hand to the Wensleydale Railway. The Michael Portillo recollection comes from Mark Rand, former Chairman of the Friends.

TUCCs - BR Closure Notices p 36-37

A third TUCC was involved. It was realised late on that a three-mile section of track between Garsdale and Ais Gill related to the TUCC for North Eastern England. Eventually, this TUCC was merged with the Yorkshire TUCC. This new body was also led by James Towler. It was after this his contract was not renewed.

Closure notices were issued under s56 of the Transport Act 1962. The one in December 1983 did not reflect the wording of the Act; the second forced BR to recognise that the notice would include eight Dales Rail stations. The final closure notice went out when it was noticed three miles of track in North East England had been omitted. Even this one was incorrect in small details.

Chapter 5 - Part 3 - Run up to the Reprieve Decision

Lazard's – Sale of Line p 40
What has now emerged is that British Rail, the Department of Transport, a Private User and Local Councils were at advanced stages of discussions in the spring of 1989. It is doubtful if this was ever viable. It is a 29-page document, including network diagram. For those interested to find out more a visit to The National Archives at Kew, London, and a request to see file AN 18/1556 Settle-Carlisle Line: correspondence relating to the proposed disposal of the line is well worth while. They will find the BR evaluation of the nine expressions of interest that had been received. This includes assessments of the working capital (very little) that each bidder had at their disposal.

Chapter 5 - Part 4 - The Final Decision - Summary and Reflections

Freight - Transport of Coal p 45
In 1985 a secret Cabinet Committee decided to move away from UK-sourced coal and to import instead. Initially this was to be transported by road. By 1990 (as this policy was to be implemented) policy makers realised that one train driver could carry the loads of 60 truck drivers. No evidence has been found that this change of policy effected the decision to refuse closure but it may have played a part in subsequent investment in the line.

Appendices

Appendix 1 - Decision making Model
Graham T Allison - Jupiter Missiles pp141-143; Blockade: p129, p134, U2 & Bomb sites pp118-123; USSR – USSR Building of Sites pp 112-113.

Appendix 2 - Significant Events 1962-1990 - Abbott and Whitehouse.

Appendix 3 - Settle-Carlisle Joint Action Committee Membership December 1988 Press Release. Funding of PEIDA Report - Abbott and Whitehouse p 68.

Appendix 4 - Settle-Carlisle Association Projects and Activities from 1990 from Edward Album and websites of the Friends, Trust and Development Company.

Appendix 5 - Settle-Carlisle Railway Freight - Engineering and Infrastructure - Capacity and Safety compiled by Roger Goode.

Appendix 8 - The two letters in this Appendix from Ruth Annison to the Prime Minister and from Edward Album to Lord Whitelaw show very different styles of advocacy. Both are quite brilliant examples of lobbying in its best sense and illustrate the great strength of the campaign.

APPENDIX 7
Illustrations

Front Cover
Portraits - Left to Right: James Allport, Margaret Thatcher, Michael Portillo, Richard Beeching.

Picture Top: Freight on Ribblehead viaduct 2014. *Courtesy Andrew Griffiths and ImageRail.*

Picture Bottom: Steam crosses Ribblehead viaduct. *Courtesy Andrew Griffiths and ImageRail.*

Page ii
Portrait: Author
Picture: 47757 "Capability Brown" on a Glasgow to Euston service crossing Ribblehead viaduct.
Courtesy of Pete Shaw.

Page iii
Map: *Courtesy of Rachel Griffiths and ImageRail.*
Wyvern Logo: Adapted for the Settle-Carlisle Line in 2010 by ImageRail.com
The Wyvern is a dragon like mythical beast and featured in the Midland Railway logo. In 2010 an new logo was developed for the group of organisations serving the line. The organisations were the Friends of the Settle-Carlisle Line, The Settle-Carlisle Railway Trust and the Settle-Carlisle Railway Development Company.

Page vii
Picture: A view of Ribblehead station. *Courtesy Andrew Griffiths and ImageRail.*

Page viii
Picture: A map of the Settle-Carlisle Line including viaduct profiles and tunnels.
Courtesy Rachel Griffiths and ImageRail.

Page 2
Picture: Carlisle Station - Black 5 44932 4-6-0 with Waverley Board. *Courtesy of Visit.Cumbria.com*

Page 3
Portrait: William Gladstone.

Page 4
Pictures: The House of Commons 1833 by Sir George Hayter. © *Permission from the National Portrait Gallery.*
Despatch box – Lord Palmerston addresses the House of Commons in debates on the Treaty of France.
(As a holder of an Irish Peerage, Lord Palmerston sat in the House of Commons for 58 years).

Page 6
Portrait: Queen Victoria.
Picture: Ingleton viaduct. *Courtesy of Jules Roberts Photography.*

Page 10
Picture Top: Gradient Profile of the Settle-Carlisle Line. The Midland Railway, Circa 1875.
Picture Bottom: Midland Railway and Scottish Joint Stock Third Class Dining Car with kitchen.

Page 14
Top Picture: Dent Head Viaduct with southbound return empty cement train, 2010.
Bottom Picture: "Tornado" crosses Smardale viaduct, 2009. *Both Courtesy of Andrew Griffiths and ImageRail.*

Page 16
Picture: 71000 "Duke of Gloucester" near Salt Lake Cottages on the Settle-Carlisle Line. *Courtesy of Pete Shaw.*

Page 18
Picture: Mallerstang Edge and Common, 2011. *Courtesy Andrew Griffiths and ImageRail.*

APPENDIX 8

Campaign Letters from Edward Album, Legal Advisor for the Friends, to Lord Whitelaw (5th Jan 1989) and Ruth Annison, Settle-Carlisle Business Liaison Group, to Mrs Thatcher (16th Jan 1989).

E.J.C.ALBUM

EJCA/AD

5th January 1989

The Rt Hon the Viscount Whitelaw, CH MC, PC, DL
House of Lords
London SW1A OPW

Dear Lord Whitelaw

SETTLE - CARLISLE LINE

I am writing on behalf of the Friends of the line and I am wondering
whether it would be possible for the Chairman of the Association and
myself to meet you in the fairly near future.

As you may have heard, we are coming close to a decision from the
Secretary of State and we are still concerned that the decision might be
to close the line. Our own view is that the case for retaining the line
has become overwhelming if we consider the following facts:-

   (a) The line is now making an operating profit and, on our
       own and on other objective forecasts, is expected to make
       an increasing profit in the years to come.

   (b) Even on the basis of British Rail's figures, the loss
       being made by the line is negligible.

   (c) A comparison between closing the line and keeping it
       open shows a balance in favour of keeping the line open.

   (d) Again, on British Rail's figures, the line covers about
       85% of its costs whereas the average for the provincial
       sector as a whole is a coverage of about 35% of the net-
       works' costs. I believe that Network South East covers
       something like 82% of its costs which shows how success-
       ful the Settle-Carlisle line is.

   (e) The line's performance has improved dramatically over
       recent years. The usage before the closure proposal was
       made in 1984 was about 90,000 passenger journeys per
       year. The current figure is about 450,000 passenger
       journeys. In fact, the line's present use for what may
       be called essential journeys is now greater than the
       total usage in 1984.

The above financial arguments leave out the major arguments of heritage
and tourism, which are as important as ever in our view.

The depth of feeling is thus very strong on the part of those campaigning to save the line and it is quite clear that, in the event of an adverse decision, the matter would be taken to the courts both by the Local Authorities and by certain individual complainants. This would be based on the issues already put to the Minister. We do not ourselves wish to threaten legal proceedings because we do not believe that this is the best way to resolve the problem.

Having recently met both the Minister and some of his officials, the impression I received is still that we are facing difficulties. Our best guess as to the reason for this is that very senior members of the Cabinet may be taking the view that the line is losing money and that British Rail should be allowed to close it. This thinking is represented by a short letter which Mr Nicholas Ridley wrote to one of his constituents, a copy of which I enclose. The facts are very different from those suggested by Mr Ridley but the original thinking may prevail. This thinking was based on much earlier statements that some £10 million – £15 million was required to repair the structures on the line (against a present estimate of under £3 million) and that the line was losing about £1 million per annum. We believe also that British Rail's most senior management have got into the frame of mind in which they are determined to close the line and have been insisting on doing so as part of their freedom to manage British Rail. Whilst we understand British Rail's approach based on the original figures, we cannot do so now.

The suggestion has been made from some ministerial quarters that the Local Authorities should, as the saying goes, "put their money where their mouth is". This suggestion, recently repeated by Mr Portillo, is that the Local Authorities should guarantee the line's revenue. This is not a reasonable suggestion because the line is owned by British Rail and is dependant for its revenue on the operating decisions which are made, including the frequency of trains, the fares charged and the connecting services.

There has been an attempt recently, as you know, to sell the line to a private owner. Our Association is not opposed to such a sale on political grounds, but we believe it to be a wrong solution for the reasons given in some detail in our Memorandum to the Department of Transport. It also looks now as if the potential bidders for the line are of insufficient substance to take on the responsibilities involved. One bidder seems to have capital and reserves of under £50,000 and the other is a newly-formed company with capital still to be raised.

The trust proposal is a very serious possibility but, as you may have seen from our Memorandum, it can only work if the decision is made to keep the line open. If such a decision were made, then, not only would the grants from English Heritage and the Local Authorities be available, but also one could launch an appeal which would have unanimous backing from all parties concerned, including the Government and British Rail.

We should be most grateful if you could spare us some time to discuss these issues and to advise us on how we might best proceed. If you were in London during the latter part of next week or during the week beginning 16th January, perhaps you could find a convenient date for a meeting. Alternatively, if preferable for you, the meeting could take place in the North of England.

Yours sincerely

Edward Album

The Prime Minister,   16th January, 1989
10, Downing Street,
London SW1A 2AA

Dear Mrs. Thatcher,

There are between one and two thousand small businesses in the Settle-
Carlisle corridor. For example, Craven has 667 businesses dependent in
whole or in part on tourism; Hawes has 105 family businesses and the
Eden Valley lists 80 tourist-related establishments.

These are reliable figures - we know because they are our friends,
neighbours and colleagues and we have counted them.

From the tea van at Ribblehead to the most upmarket hotel where your
ministers dine, from estate agents to shops in market towns, from
village post offices to manufacturers, all agree the Settle-Carlisle
railway should be kept open. 'Open' means more than mere survival as a
summer season fun railway. OPEN means, at the very least, continuation
of the present level of all-year passenger and Red Star parcel services.

60% of the passengers on the Settle-Carlisle line are said to be
travelling "for pleasure." 60% of the passenger journeys in 1988 meant
up to 150,000 people, all wanting to eat and be entertained, to shop and
often to sleep overnight in the area. Cafes and craft shops, information
centres and youth hostels, hotels, petrol stations and holiday cottage
owners, all know these passengers because they meet them face-to-face.

Also grateful for these customers are the plumbers who put new bathrooms
into hotels to provide en-suite facilities; milkmen, butchers, bakers
and greengrocers who supply restaurants; the brewers; the designers and
printers of postcards, maps and leisure guides; and many, many others,
because of the remarkable ripple effect of tourism on the local economy.

      SOME OF THESE PEOPLE DESCRIBE IN THIS BOOK WHAT CLOSURE OF THE
      LINE WOULD MEAN TO THEM. WE HAVE HAD 16 YEARS WITHOUT STATIONS
      OR TRAINS AND THEREFORE FIRST-HAND EXPERIENCE OF THE PROBLEMS.

Since eight stations were re-opened in 1986 our situation has been
transformed - and continues to improve. Any change in ownership and
management of the line which does not guarantee the long-term security
of the present level of year-round services would threaten jobs, the
rural economy and the well-being of communities through which the line
passes (four Parliamentary constituencies, including Richmond).

Yours sincerely,

Ruth Annison

Mrs. Ruth Annison
on behalf of THE SETTLE-CARLISLE RAILWAY BUSINESS LIAISON GROUP

c/o W.R.Outhwaite and Son, Ropemakers, Hawes, N. Yorkshire. DL8 3NT
     Telephone (09697) 487 and 676

APPENDIX 9

Paul Channon letter 6th April 1989 to the Prime Minister Civil Service Final Assessment to Michael Portillo

PRIME MINISTER

SETTLE-CARLISLE RAILWAY

I have now completed my review of the available evidence about the proposed closure of the historic Settle-Carlisle line. As you know, this is a difficult case which has aroused strong emotions. It has dragged on for over 5 years. I have concluded that I should, after all, refuse British Rail consent to close the line.

Last May, I announced that I was minded to agree that the line should close to British Rail passenger services. The private sector were invited to bid for the line. And in order to limit the grounds for legal challenge, I deferred a final decision to give objectors an opportunity to provide fresh evidence. I have now received some important new evidence which affects the case for closure.

The financial case for closure is now significantly less robust and hence more dependent on judgment. More people are using the line so there is higher revenue; and the costs are lower than originally estimated. The details are set out in the attached Annex. The balance of probability in my view is that in BR's ownership the line will continue to run at a small annual loss of perhaps £500,000. On slightly more optimistic assumptions, particularly on revenue, the line could make a small annual profit of about £100,000.

There are a number of other considerations which I have had to bear in mind in coming to a decision, such as the hardship case, tourism and the wider economic benefits of retaining the line. These are explored more fully in the Annex. I do not believe that these factors are in themselves strong reasons for retaining the line but they do need to be considered in conjunction with the weaker financial case. The local authorities attach great weight to them and to the increase in traffic on the line and have made it clear they would seek judicial review of a closure decision. Given the changes in the financial case I am less confident that we would win the case. I am also doubtful about the wisdom of antagonising many in the North of England for such small and uncertain savings. I believe that this doubt is shared by most of our colleagues in the House.

BR have made considerable efforts to privatise the line.
There have been a number of bids but none had sufficient
financial backing. So, even if I wanted to close the line to
BR, there would be little chance of an early and successful
privatisation. Nevertheless, I feel strongly that the
interest shown by the private sector is evidence that this
line could be financially viable if energetically and
enthusiastically marketed. I shall insist that BR involve
the private sector in its future. The public interest shown
in the line suggests also that fares could be increased to
reflect the value to users. I shall press BR on that. There
has been widespread support among the line's supporters for
the idea of a Trust to raise funds for the preservation of
Ribblehead Viaduct and other historic structures on the
line. I propose to encourage this. These initiatives
together with contributions which have been promised by
public bodies will, I hope, go a long way to improving the
line's finances.

Presentation will need careful handling but I can reconcile
our approach with our previous announcement that I was
minded to agree to closure: I can point to the various
changes in the case for closure. I also believe that the
decision will not affect the progress of our bus
substitution policy: indeed a number of cases are in the
pipeline.

Subject to any views which you or other colleagues may have,
I propose to make the announcement on Tuesday, 11 April. I
enclose the text of my Written Parliamentary Answer. My
officials will then issue a formal decision letter to BR.

Copies of this minute go to the Secretaries of State for
Employment, the Environment and Trade and Industry, the
Minister of Agriculture, the Chief Secretary, the
Attorney-General, the Leader of the House, the Lord Privy
Seal, the Chief Whip and Sir Robin Butler.

P. C.

PAUL CHANNON
6 April 1989

SETTLE-CARLISLE RAILWAY

Background

Last May, following consultations with you and other colleagues, Sir David Mitchell announced that I was minded to agree that the line should close to British Rail passenger services. There seemed to be a financial case for closure; we thought that the provision of substitute bus services, guaranteed by BR, would cater for the overwhelming majority of passengers travelling for essential transport purposes much more cheaply; and that most of the line's passengers were using it for leisure purposes, the majority of whom were travelling simply for the pleasure of the ride. But in order to limit the grounds for legal challenge, I deferred a final decision to give objectors an opportunity to provide fresh evidence. At the same time, the private sector were invited to bid for the line. Predictably, there was a storm of protest. However, I have received some important new evidence which affects the case for closure.

Revised Financial Case

The main change is that the financial case for closure is significantly less robust and dependent on more finely balanced judgment. The available evidence suggests that the annual number of trips on the line has risen by at least 50%, from about 300,000 in 1986 to over 450,000 in 1988. This has increased the revenue generated by the line by 40%. Actual revenue is now towards the top of the range in BR's financial case rather than at the lower end as previously. Some of this traffic may have been generated by the fear of closure. But the attraction of the line to tourists is clear and there must be great potential if it is well marketed. At the same time the estimates of cost have changed primarily because trial repairs to Ribblehead Viaduct have shown that it would cost less to repair. BR engineers had originally estimated a range of £2.7m - £4.3m. Their revised estimate is now £3m, but English

Heritage think that it may cost as little as £2m. The major
area of uncertainty is how much revenue the line can
generate. My economists have looked carefully at BR's
revised financial case and firmly recommend a number of
further revisions which together produce a potential annual
loss ranging from £0.2m to £1m (£1.9m to £9.7m in Net
Present Value terms discounted over 15 years). If one adds
in contributions of £1.6m already promised from English
Heritage, local authorities and the Rural Development
Commission and assumes a small increase in revenue at the
top end of the range possibly as low as 2%, then on
optimistic assumptions the line would show a small profit.
The balance of probability in my view is that in BR
ownership it will continue to run at a loss, but probably
not a large one, and it is very much a question of
judgment. Better marketing and increased fares would have a
significant impact.

Hardship and Wider Economic Considerations
There are other considerations which I have had to bear in
mind in coming to a decision. Of the higher traffic level
referred to above, the evidence suggests that about 100,000
journeys in 1988 were for essential transport purposes such
as work, education, and shopping. It seems that
significantly more people are now using it for day-to-day
purposes. And there are signs that more may do so if the
line's future is secured. Although the number of essential
trips has increased, I still do not believe that closing the
line would cause serious hardship to many people, but the
hardship case is marginally stronger than it was. I still
believe that the provision of a substitute bus service would
be feasible, although it would not provide as comprehensive
or convenient a service as the train.

It is quite in line with our rail subsidy policy to support
rail services where communities are economically dependent
on them. Many objectors (including local businesses and
Chambers of Commerce) argue that closing the line would have
a devastating effect on the local economy. Much of the

evidence is anecdotal. However, the line's importance to
the local economy has been recently confirmed by the Rural
Development Commission and a new report, commissioned from
consultants by the English Tourist Board, suggests that over
300 existing and new jobs (including railway employees)
could be supported by the line if it stays open and is fully
developed and marketed.

Of course, if the line closes, expenditure by tourists and
taxpayers will be released for other purposes and some of
these jobs may well be generated elsewhere in the
economy. The Settle-Carlisle corridor is not in any case an
area of particularly high unemployment. But there is no
doubt that it has great tourism potential. If the line goes
and it is no longer so easy to visit the area, expenditure
by tourists (especially those from overseas) may be directed
to other popular, but overcrowded, resorts where the
benefits of that expenditure may be offset by the disbenefit
of increased tourist congestion. Alternatively, those
visitors may direct their expenditure to other countries.

Privatisation

Legal advice is that the closure decision should not take
into account the possibility of future private sector
operation of the line after closure, as under present
legislation this could not be guaranteed. It is clear that
the economic benefits generated by the line, particularly
tourism, would be maintained and possibly increased if the
line could be successfully privatised. BR have made
considerable efforts to achieve privatisation. But, although
a number of bids were received, only one has been worth
considering because of the need for extensive financial
backing. In recent days it has become clear that even this
bid is unsatisfactory. Although the bid is in principle
supported by a major backer (Brent Walker), the backer is
not prepared to give a sufficient financial guarantee until
a feasibility study has been completed and planning consents
from the very local authorities who oppose closure have been

obtained for various leisure developments. And the bidder
is seeking various open-ended commitments from BR which
would be quite unacceptable both to BR and to us. In short,
I see no chance that negotiations can be completed quickly
and successfully. If I were to decide to close the line, it
would be very unlikely that a private operator could or
would be prepared to take it on in the near future.

Nevertheless, I still feel strongly that the private sector
should have a role in developing the line. The interest that
the private sector have shown is ample evidence of the
line's potential. It is also evidence that travellers may be
prepared to pay substantially more than the BR fare. The
local authorities have also promised to co-operate with BR
and other organisations (including private sector firms) to
develop the line if closure consent is refused. They have
already made various constructive proposals, such as the
setting up of a trust to raise funds, in particular for the
repair of Ribblehead Viaduct. I shall press BR to set up
joint ventures with the private sector and I shall encourage
the formation of a trust.

Bus substitution
We need to consider the effect of a decision to refuse
closure consent on our bus substitution policy and also how
such a decision should be presented in view of my previous
statement that I was minded to close the line. It could be
argued that a decision to refuse closure in this case might
be a disincentive to BR to bring forward further closure
proposals though the Chairman of BR does not make that
connection. I am confident that we can make good progress
on bus substitution. The Board are working on a number of
proposals where the financial case is very much more clear
cut. The senior management of the Board are in no doubt that
we are committed to this policy.

From: J R COATES
       Railways
Date: 24 February 1989

1.   PS/ Mr Portillo

2.   PS/Secretary of State

Copies (with draft minute to Prime Minister only)

PS/Secretary of State (advance copy)
PS/Mr Bottomley
PS/Lord Brabazon   **Copies (with Annexes I-XII**
Mr Ballard - YHRO   **but without other documents)**
Mr Kendall - NWRO
Miss Buchanan   PS/Sir Alan Bailey
Mr Grimsey   Mr Palmer
Miss Lambert   Mr Beetham
Mr Reeves   Mr H M G Stevens
Miss Samuel   Mr Peal
Mr Holmes   Mr Cunliffe
                                    Mr Fairclough
                                    Mrs Chipping

TRANSPORT ACTS 1962 AND 1968: BRITISH RAILWAYS BOARD:
PROPOSED WITHDRAWAL OF PASSENGER TRAIN SERVICES BETWEEN:

(a)   SETTLE JUNCTION AND CARLISLE (PETTERIL BRIDGE JUNCTION)
AND
      FROM INTERMEDIATE STATIONS

AND

(b)   BLACKBURN (DAISYFIELD JUNCTION) AND HELLIFIELD AND FROM
      CLITHEROE STATION

Introduction: Summary

1.   This submission makes recommendations about BR's proposed
withdrawal of all passenger services between Settle Junction
and Carlisle, and between Hellifield and Blackburn. (The latter
line is at present only open because it is used for summer
excursion trains on their way to and from the Settle- Carlisle
line. The decision on whether or not this line stays open depends
entirely on the fate of Settle-Carlisle. So this submission

RB1/89

APPENDIX 10

Notices of Reprieve

Department of Transport Letter to British Railways Board

Department of Transport
Room   S19/14A
2 Marsham Street London SW1P 3EB
Telex 22221 Direct line 01-212 276 4820
Switchboard 01-212 3434
GTN 212

The Secretary
British Railways Board
Euston House
24 Eversholt Street   11 April 1989
London
NW1 2DZ

Sir

PROPOSAL TO WITHDRAW RAIL PASSENGER SERVICES BETWEEN SETTLE
JUNCTION AND CARLISLE (PETTERIL BRIDGE JUNCTION); AND BETWEEN
BLACKBURN (DAISYFIELD JUNCTION) AND HELLIFIELD

1.   I am directed by the Secretary of State for Transport, to
refer to the proposal published by the British Railways Board in
accordance with Section 56 of the Transport Act 1962 to withdraw
all their railway passenger services between Settle Junction and
Carlisle (Petteril Bridge Junction); and between Blackburn
(Daisyfield Junction) and Hellifield; and to close the stations at
Settle, Horton-in-Ribblesdale, Ribblehead, Dent, Garsdale, Kirkby
Stephen, Appleby, Langwathby, Lazonby and Kirkoswald, Armathwaite
and Clitheroe.

2.   The Secretary of State has carefully considered all relevant
factors and has decided to refuse consent to the Board's
proposal.

Objections to the Closure Proposal

3.   The Transport Users Consultative Committees for North East
and North Western England have considered over 32,000 objections
to the closure proposal and have made joint reports to the
Secretary of State on the hardship which closure would cause. The
Secretary of State has directly received submissions from the

Joint Councils Steering Committee, representing the local
authorities in the area, Committee and the Friends of the
Settle-Carlisle Line Association representing various groups
supporting the Line; from the Business Liaison Group and Chambers
of Commerce representing local businesses; and from other
organisations. He also directly received over 6,500 objections
from individuals and a petition against closure with over 40,000
signatures. The Secretary of State is grateful to all those who
have submitted evidence to him.

The Financial Case for Closure

4.   The Secretary of State has carefully considered the Board's
initial financial case and their revised case along with all the
representations made to him about them. In his view the balance of
probability is that the line will continue to run at a loss, but
not necessarily a large one: it is very much a question of
judgement.

5.   Future revenue is the major area of uncertainty. A recent
survey has identified a significant growth in traffic and actual
revenue tends to confirm that. The attraction of the
Settle-Carlisle line to tourists is clear and there should be
scope for increasing revenue further if the line is fully
developed and marketed with the Board charging fares on a more
commercial basis. At the same time estimates of cost have changed,
notably those for repairing the Ribblehead Viaduct which have been
reduced. In his assessment of the Board's revised case, the
Secretary of State has left aside the proposed alternative rail
service via Carnforth. If he were to give closure consent for the
Settle-Carlisle Line, he would not require the Board to run this
alternative service as a means of relieving hardship because it is
already possible to make the journey between Leeds and Carlisle
via the West Coast Main Line.

6.   Financial contributions towards the cost of repairing
Ribblehead Viaduct, subject to certain conditions, have been
offered by English Heritage (up to £1m or 40% of eligible costs,
whichever is the less), £500,000 by the local authorities and

2

Department of Transport Letter to British Railways Board

£100,000 by the Rural Development Commission. Building materials
at a reduced price may be available from member firms of the
British Aggregate Construction Materials Industries and the
Federation of Resin Formulators and Applicators. And the Friends
of the Settle-Carlisle Line Association, supported by the local
authorities, have proposed a trust to raise funds for the line's
structures. Such contributions together with new marketing
initiatives would all help to improve the line's finances.

Hardship
7.   The Secretary of State has taken careful account of the
report on hardship submitted by the Transport Users Consultative
Committees in 1986 and their further report submitted in 1988. He
accepts that closure of the Settle-Carlisle line would cause some
hardship to local residents who now rely on it for day-to-day,
essential transport purposes. He considers that provision of
guaranteed substitute bus services could cater adequately for many
such travellers. The recent survey suggests that about 100,000
journeys in 1988 were for essential purposes. He accepts that the
hardship case for retaining the line is now marginally stronger
than it was, but does not believe that hardship in itself would
justify retaining the line.

8.   The Secretary of State does not accept that closure would
cause serious hardship to other categories of users. In
particular, the Secretary of State does not agree with the TUCCs'
view that closure would cause considerable hardship to tourists
and rail enthusiasts who would be deprived of the pleasure of
using the line.

Wider Social and Economic Considerations
9.   Many objectors (including local businesses and Chambers of
Commerce) have made new representations that closing the line
would have a serious effect on the local economy. The line's
importance to the local economy has been recently confirmed by the
Rural Development Commission and a report commissioned by the
English Tourist Board. The Secretary of State has noted all these
views and representations.

3

The Secretary of State's Decision

10. The Secretary of State, in exercise of his powers under Section 56 of the Transport Act 1962 and Section 54 of the Transport Act 1968, having taken into account the Board's case, the Transport Users Consultative Committees' reports on hardship and all other relevant factors including social and economic considerations, hereby refuses consent to the withdrawal of all rail passenger services between Settle Junction and Carlisle (Petteril Bridge Junction) and between Blackburn (Daisyfield Junction) and Hellifield. He also refuses consent to the closure to the Board's services of the stations at Settle, Horton-in-Ribblesdale, Ribblehead, Dent, Garsdale, Kirkby Stephen, Appleby, Langwathby, Lazonby and Kirkoswald, Armathwaite and Clitheroe.

Next Steps

11. The Secretary of State welcomes the interest shown in the line by the private sector and the commitment of the local authorities and other organisations to supporting the line if it stays open. He now asks the Board urgently to explore the scope for drawing on the skills of the private sector, to ensure a successful future for the line at a minimum cost to public funds. He also wishes the Board vigorously to develop a new marketing strategy charging fares on a more commercial basis. He now looks to all interested parties to work together to ensure that the line has a successful future and so that the case for closure will not re-emerge.

I am, Sir,
Your obedient servant

R S PEAL
An Assistant Secretary in
the Department of Transport

81

MINISTER
FOR PUBLIC TRANSPORT

DEPARTMENT OF TRANSPORT
2 MARSHAM STREET LONDON SW1P 3EB

My ref:

Your ref:

Mr E J C Album
Gotch House
20-34 St Bride Street
London
EC4A 4DL

11 APR 1989

Dear Mr Album

You will be pleased to hear that the Secretary of State is today announcing that he is refusing consent for British Rail to close the Settle-Carlisle railway line. I enclose a copy of the Department's Press Notice and the formal decision letter.

I look to the Friends of the Settle-Carlisle Line Association to co-operate vigorously in supporting and promoting the line, as you have promised.

Yours sincerely

Michael Portillo.

MICHAEL PORTILLO

COMING SHORTLY

HOW THE LINE WAS SAVED

Additional Documents
by
Martin Pearson

Joining the Friends of the Settle - Carlisle Line

You can use this page to join FoSCL.
Please complete the details below and send with your cheque to:

SCRDC (FoSCL membership), Railway Station, Clifford Street, Appleby, CA16 6TT

For telephone enquiries please call:
Phone: 017683 53200 or
Email: membership@settle-carlisle.com

or alternatively apply online at **www.foscl.org.uk**

Please tick category:

Junior Member	☐ £3		**Individual Member**	☐ £10
Family Member	☐ £12.50		**Corporate Member**	☐ £40
Life Member	☐ £250		**Joint Life Member**	☐ £350
European Member	☐ £20		**Rest of the World**	☐ £25

Total payment of £ _____   (Please make cheques payable to 'FoSCL')

**Your Name
(BLOCK CAPITALS)** _____

Address _____

Town _____

Postcode _____

Phone _____

email _____

Landslip at Eden Brows
on the Settle - Carlisle Line

Following the dramatic heavy rains over Christmas and New Year of 2015/2016 a portion of the embankment at Eden Brows near Carlisle started to move. By February 2016 the movement was considered so serious that the Line was closed. Network Rail are, at the time of writing, undertaking significant repairs to the embankment, including the drilling and insertion of giant rods into the rock below the track formation to give secure platform for the railway above. This work is expected to take a year.

The picture above shows 6L62 Eden Brows-Kingmoor Yard spoil train approaching Howe & Co running wrong direction, on the Up Line. At Howe & Co it will use the crossover to get onto the Down line, and then exit the Engineers possession.

66092 (furthest from the camera) leads the train of 40 Coalfish wagons, conveying almost 1,600 tonnes of spoil, with 66108 dead on the rear. This loco had brought the train on site the previous day. Only about a dozen of these trains ran.

Time 0745, date 24/08/16.

Photographer: Rachel Griffiths. Train driver: Andrew Griffiths